A CENSUS THAT MIRRORS AMERICA

Interim Report

Panel to Evaluate Alternative Census Methods

Committee on National Statistics

Commission on Behavioral and Social Sciences and Education

National Research Council

NATIONAL ACADEMY PRESS
Washington, D.C. 1993

NOTICE: The project that is the subject of this report was approved by the Governing Board of the National Research Council, whose members are drawn from the councils of the National Academy of Sciences, the National Academy of Engineering, and the Institute of Medicine. The members of the committee responsible for the report were chosen for their special competences and with regard for appropriate balance.

This report has been reviewed by a group other than the authors according to procedures approved by a Report Review Committee consisting of members of the National Academy of Sciences, the National Academy of Engineering, and the Institute of Medicine.

The National Academy of Sciences is a private, nonprofit, self-perpetuating society of distinguished scholars engaged in scientific and engineering research, dedicated to the furtherance of science and technology and to their use for the general welfare. Upon the authority of the charter granted to it by the Congress in 1863, the Academy has a mandate that requires it to advise the federal government on scientific and technical matters. Dr. Bruce M. Alberts is president of the National Academy of Sciences.

The National Academy of Engineering was established in 1964, under the charter of the National Academy of Sciences, as a parallel organization of outstanding engineers. It is autonomous in its administration and in the selection of its members, sharing with the National Academy of Sciences the responsibility for advising the federal government. The National Academy of Engineering also sponsors engineering programs aimed at meeting national needs, encourages education and research, and recognizes the superior achievements of engineers. Dr. Robert M. White is president of the National Academy of Engineering.

The Institute of Medicine was established in 1970 by the National Academy of Sciences to secure the services of eminent members of appropriate professions in the examination of policy matters pertaining to the health of the public. The Institute acts under the responsibility given to the National Academy of Sciences by its congressional charter to be an adviser to the federal government and, upon its own initiative, to identify issues of medical care, research, and education. Dr. Kenneth I. Shine is president of the Institute of Medicine.

The National Research Council was organized by the National Academy of Sciences in 1916 to associate the broad community of science and technology with the Academy's purposes of furthering knowledge and advising the federal government. Functioning in accordance with general policies determined by the Academy, the Council has become the principal operating agency of both the National Academy of Sciences and the National Academy of Engineering in providing services to the government, the public, and the scientific and engineering communities. The Council is administered jointly by both Academies and the Institute of Medicine. Dr. Bruce M. Alberts and Dr. Robert M. White are chairman and vice chairman, respectively, of the National Research Council.

This project is supported by funds provided by the Bureau of the Census, U.S. Department of Commerce, under contract number 50-YABC-1-66032.

Library of Congress Catalog Card No. 93-85916
International Standard Book Number 0-309-04979-2

Additional copies of this report are available from:

National Academy Press
2101 Constitution Avenue, N.W.
Box 285
Washington, D.C. 20055

Call 800-624-6242 or 202-334-3313 (in the Washington Metropolitan Area).

B206

A Census That Mirrors America

Interim Report

PANEL TO EVALUATE ALTERNATIVE CENSUS METHODS

NORMAN M. BRADBURN (*Chair*), National Opinion Research Center, University of Chicago

ROBERT M. BELL, The RAND Corporation, Santa Monica, California

GORDON J. BRACKSTONE, Statistics Canada, Ottawa, Ontario

CLIFFORD C. CLOGG, Department of Sociology and Department of Statistics, Pennsylvania State University

THOMAS B. JABINE, statistical consultant, Washington, D.C.

KATHERINE S. NEWMAN, Department of Anthropology, Columbia University

D. BRUCE PETRIE, Statistics Canada, Ottawa, Ontario

PETER A. ROGERSON, Department of Geography, State University of New York, Buffalo

KEITH F. RUST, Westat, Inc., Rockville, Maryland

NORA CATE SCHAEFFER, Department of Sociology, University of Wisconsin

EDWARD A. SCHILLMOELLER, A.C. Nielsen Company, Northbrook, Illinois

MICHAEL F. WEEKS, Research Triangle Institute, Research Triangle Park, North Carolina

ALAN M. ZASLAVSKY, Department of Statistics, Harvard University

DUANE L. STEFFEY, *Study Director*

ANU PEMMARAZU, *Senior Project Assistant*

CONTENTS

PREFACE

In response to the Decennial Census Improvement Act of 1991 and at the request of the U.S. Department of Commerce and the Bureau of the Census, the National Research Council in 1992 began two studies on the census in the year 2000. The studies are being conducted by two panels under the Research Council's Committee on National Statistics (CNSTAT). One study, being conducted by the Panel on Census Requirements in the Year 2000 and Beyond, is considering what purposes a decennial census serves and whether alternative data collection systems can meet these objectives. The interim report of that panel was published earlier this year (Committee on National Statistics, 1993); its final report is scheduled for completion in late 1994.

The second study, being conducted by the Panel to Evaluate Alternative Census Methods, is focusing on *how* the census should be taken. The panel includes members with expertise in statistics, survey methods and design, decennial census operations, field organization of large-scale data collection, demography, geography, marketing research, administrative records and record linkage, small-area statistics, and respondent behavior (see the Appendix).

The panel transmitted its first report to the Census Bureau in December 1992 (Commiteee on National Statistics, 1992). That letter report offered general comments on the design selection process and made several recommendations regarding further consideration of the use of administrative records for the nation's censuses in the future. This interim report presents our findings and conclusions to date, many of which concern the 1995 census test. Our final report is scheduled to be completed in spring 1994.

The panel has conducted much of its work through four groups that were formed to consider different aspects of alternative census designs: (1) sampling and statistical estimation; (2) response and coverage issues, including alternative enumeration methods; (3) administrative records; and (4) minimal content and multi-stage designs.

Robert Bell serves as convenor for the first working group, which also includes Clifford Clogg and Alan Zaslavsky. This group is examining how problems of coverage and differential coverage can be assessed and improved with sampling and statistical estimation methods. Topics under investigation by this group include sampling and truncation of nonresponse follow-up operations and alternative coverage measurement methodologies, including integrated coverage measurement techniques designed to yield a "one-number" census. This working group was primarily responsible for drafting Chapter 2 of this interim report.

Nora Cate Schaeffer serves as convenor for the second working group, which also includes Katherine Newman and Michael Weeks. This group is examining response and coverage issues and reviewing research on methods to improve census response and reduce differential coverage. Topics under study by the group include questionnaire design and implementation, multiple response modes, census outreach and promotion, ethnographic research, research on living situations, and census residence rules. The working group was primarily responsible for drafting Chapter 3 of this interim report.

Thomas Jabine serves as convenor of the third working group, which also includes Gordon Brackstone and Peter Rogerson. This group has been studying current and potential uses of administrative records in censuses and other components of the Census Bureau's demographic data systems. The working group is considering technical, legal, and administrative issues--as well as factors such as cost and public acceptability--regarding new uses of administrative records and future research and development. The working group was primarily responsible for drafting Chapter 4 of this interim report.

Keith Rust serves as convenor for the fourth working group, which also includes Bruce Petrie, Edward Schillmoeller, and Norman Bradburn. This group is examining census designs that involve either minimal data content or data collection over a decade. The working group's agenda includes designs that depart from the tradition of asking all census questions on April 1. The group is considering both technical and nontechnical issues associated with the implementation of these designs. This working group had primary responsibility for drafting Chapter 5 of this interim report.

The primary audience for this interim report is the Census Bureau, but we have also tried to include sufficient technical background so that the report is accessible to a wider audience. We intend to revisit these topics and our recommendations as new and relevant information becomes available during the life of the panel.

The panel has endeavored to deliver a timely interim report. We have offered a generous number of recommendations, and we hope the Census Bureau will find this interim report useful in planning for the 1995 census test. At the time of this writing, plans are still relatively early in development. We believe that, if properly designed and executed, one major contribution of the 1995 census test will be cost data on the innovations under consideration--e.g., nonresponse follow-up sampling and truncation, application of the targeting model and tool kit, and new approaches to coverage measurement. Accurate information on cost and operational effectiveness will be essential for making sound decisions in December 1995, based on the results of the census tests, regarding the final design for the 2000 census.

We have not attempted in this interim report to assign explicit priorities among our recommendations, although some have shorter timetables for action and, therefore, greater urgency. After further deliberation and review of forthcoming results from the 2000 census research and development program, we expect in our final report to assess the relative importance of different activities related to 2000 census design and implementation.

final report to assess the relative importance of different activities related to 2000 census design and implementation.

We thank the Census Bureau staff for their accessibility and cooperation in providing information and materials for deliberations of our panel and its working groups. At the first meeting of the panel, we were pleased to be addressed by Barbara Everitt Bryant, then director of the Census Bureau, and Harry Scarr, current acting director of the Census Bureau. We would like to give special thanks to Robert Tortora, Susan Miskura, and Mary Mulry for providing regular briefings on 2000 census research and for responding promptly to requests for documentation. Also, we thank the following members of the Year 2000 Research and Development Staff who were extremely generous with their time: Solomona Aoelua, Bob Bair, LaVerne Collins, Arthur Cresce, Jim Dinwiddie, Catherine Keeley, Jay Keller, Joe Knott, Charlene Leggieri, Sandy Lucas, and Violetta Vasquez. Other Census Bureau staff with whom the panel consulted include Charles Alexander, Leslie Brownrigg, Tom DeCair, Gregg Diffendal, Don Dillman, Jerry Gates, Deborah Griffin, Susan Knight, John Long, Elizabeth Martin, Laurie Moyer, and Signe Wetrogan. We are impressed by their unconstrained vision in exploring alternative census designs that represent fundamental change from traditional methods, and we look forward to continuing our work in fulfilling the panel's mission with their encouragement and support.

Federal agency representatives who provided information include Chris Mihm and Bruce Johnson of the U.S. General Accounting Office, Katherine Wallman of the U.S. Office of Management and Budget, and Fritz Scheuren, Ellen Yau, and Peter Sailer of the Internal Revenue Service. The panel is also grateful for discussions with several congressional staff members, including TerriAnn Lowenthal, Shelly Wilkie Martinez, and David McMillen.

There are many staff members of the Committee on National Statistics who provided guidance and advice, particularly Miron Straf, Constance Citro, Barry Edmonston, Edwin Goldfield, and Meyer Zitter. The panel also appreciates the editorial work of Eugenia Grohman, associate director for reports of the Commission on Behavioral and Social Sciences and Education. Her suggestions greatly improved the report's structure and presentation.

We especially thank our panel staff. Anu Pemmarazu imperturbably managed the often challenging logistics of panel meetings, competently handled the preparation of various report drafts and panel minutes, and resolved a myriad of administrative matters with efficiency and professionalism. Most of all, we are indebted to Duane Steffey, who has borne much of the burden of keeping us on track, providing working drafts, and synthesizing our prose into a readable and integrated document.

Finally, I would like to thank the panel members for their generous contribution of time and expert knowledge. I look forward to continued work with the panel.

Norman M. Bradburn, *Chair*
Panel to Evaluate Alternative
Census Methods

EXECUTIVE SUMMARY

Two major criticisms were levelled against the 1990 census: (1) unit costs increased significantly, continuing a trend that began with the 1970 census; (2) the problem of differential undercount by race persisted and even worsened, despite a large investment in coverage improvement programs (see, e.g., U.S. General Accounting Office, 1992). In response to these criticisms, the Census Bureau is considering an unprecedented level of innovation for the 2000 census.

In this interim report we concentrate on those aspects of census methodology that have the greatest effect on these two primary objectives of census redesign: reducing differential undercount and controlling costs. Therefore, we focus on processes for the collection of data, the quality of coverage and response that these processes engender, and the use of sampling (and subsequent estimation) in the collection process.

Census data collection involves four key steps: (1) the construction of an address frame; (2) an initial process to obtain responses that can be linked to the address frame; (3) a follow-up process to obtain responses from those not covered in the initial process; and (4) a coverage assessment process that estimates the size of the population not covered through the initial and follow-up processes. In the 1990 and earlier censuses, the first three steps led to the official census estimates; whether or not to incorporate the estimates from the fourth step into the official census estimates became the "adjustment issue." For the 2000 census, the Census Bureau is proposing a fundamentally different approach, called a "one-number census." The one-number census describes an approach that regards this fourth step as an integral part of the census process that leads to the official estimates.

The design of a census data collection process in essence amounts to deciding which methods of identification, enumeration, response, and coverage improvement should be applied at each of the steps; whether sampling methods (and the corresponding estimation methods) should be used at any of the four steps; and if sampling methods are used, which methods and at which steps. These decisions have to be based on information about the effectiveness and costs of the various alternative methods. The 1995 census test should be a prime source of such information.

In this report we present 35 recommendations that address a broad range of issues with varying degrees of complexity and urgency. Below we present the recommendations organized by the primary intended audience and the associated time frame. (The numbering below follows that of the body of the report.) All but 2 of our recommendations are directed to the Census Bureau, 15 are specifically directed toward the 1995 census test, and 18 are directed toward longer range issues.

ADDRESS LIST DEVELOPMENT AND
USE OF ADMINISTRATIVE DATA

Of the two recommendations not directed to the Census Bureau, one calls for congressional action to facilitate cooperative efforts at address list development.

Recommendation 1.3: Congress should enact legislation that permits the sharing of address lists between the Census Bureau and the U.S. Postal Service for the purpose of improving the Census Bureau's master address file.

The second recommendation asks the Office of Management and Budget to assume greater responsibility for statistical uses of administrative records.

Recommendation 4.1: The Statistical Policy Office in the Office of Management and Budget should recognize statistical uses of administrative records as one of its major areas of responsibility and should assume an active role in facilitating more effective working relationships between statistical and program agencies and in tracking relevant legislation.

ONE-NUMBER CENSUS

One key message is that the dual objectives of reducing the differential undercount and controlling costs will require expanded use of sampling and statistical estimation. This theme is prominent in the recommendations regarding the development and testing of coverage measurement methods.

Recommendation 2.3: We endorse the Census Bureau's stated goal of achieving a one-number census in 2000 that incorporates the results from coverage measurement programs, including programs involving sampling and statistical estimation, into the offical census population totals. We recommend that research on alternative methodologies continue in pursuit of this goal.

THE 1995 CENSUS TEST

Many of our recommendations address the 1995 census test, including preliminary research that would inform the design of the test.

Coverage Measurement

Recommendation 2.4: Before final design of the 1995 census test, the Census Bureau should critically evaluate the SuperCensus method of coverage measurement by using 1990 data to learn whether adequately precise coverage estimates are possible using ratios to the housing base.

Recommendation 2.5: Development and testing methodology for the Post-Enumeration Survey (PES) should continue in parallel with other methods until another method proves superior in operational tests. All methods still under consideration--including the PES--should be evaluated critically against common criteria.

Sampling

We call for experimentation in the 1995 census test with the use of sampling to follow up people who do not respond to the initial mail questionnaire and to collect additional information on the census form.

Recommendation 2.1: The Census Bureau should continue research on nonresponse follow-up sampling and truncation, including consideration of a combined strategy with a truncated first stage and sampling during a second stage of follow-up. Evaluation should consider effects of the nonresponse follow-up design on costs and on variance at a variety of geographic levels, from states to small areas.

Recommendation 2.7: The Census Bureau should continue research on possible matrix sampling designs, using the 1990 census data to simulate tabulations and crosstabulations. Design(s) that appear most promising should be tested in 1995 to permit evaluation of their performance in combination with other census design features under test.

Questionnaire Design and Telephone Follow-Up

We make several recommendations with respect to questionnaire design and implementation in the 1995 census test, including use of the telephone to contact persons who do not respond to the initial mailing.

Recommendation 3.1: At this time, the Census Bureau should not initiate any further large-scale experiments designed to improve the initial mail response rate. Instead, response improvement research should now consolidate findings from research conducted to date in order to design experiments for the 1995 census test. The primary objective of these experiments should be to identify optimal field procedures that combine features such as advance notification, replacement questionnaires, and telephone follow-up.

Recommendation 3.2: The prospect of having telephone numbers for a large percentage of households in the 2000 census is a potentially important development that should be explored in the Census Bureau's 1995 test--for example, by using the telephone for reminder calls and nonresponse follow-up.

Recommendation 3.12: When developing and applying residence rules, the Census Bureau should consider both the need to accurately enumerate diverse household structures and the potential for mode effects when an instrument is implemented in both self-administered and interviewer-administered forms. In particular, the Census Bureau should simultaneously develop enumeration forms designed for self-administration and telephone administration for use in the 1995 census test. The comparability of these forms should subsequently be evaluated on the basis of 1995 census test results.

Outreach and Promotion

The panel believes that greater attention should be given to census outreach and promotion and to enumeration methods targeted at historically hard-to-count segments of population. In particular, testing of candidate programs and methods should take place in 1995.

Recommendation 3.5: The Census Bureau should establish an ongoing research and development program for decennial census outreach and promotion. The 1995 census test provides an excellent opportunity to conduct and evaluate promising media campaigns and local outreach programs.

Recommendation 3.8: The Census Bureau should consider developing an extensive network of relations between field offices and local community resources. This infrastructure would be maintained in continuous operation between and during census years. The Census Bureau should develop and implement pilot programs in conjunction with the 1995 census test in order to gather information about the potential costs and benefits of a large-scale local outreach program.

Recommendation 3.10: In the 1995 census test, the Census Bureau should evaluate specific measures and procedures that might improve the enumeration of historically undercounted populations. Candidates for study in 1995 should include a larger repertoire of foreign-language materials (both written and audio), more aggressive hiring of community-based enumerators, and greater flexibility in the timing of enumeration (i.e., contact during evenings and weekends). In particular, the Census Bureau should examine the efficacy of moving census day to the middle of the month.

Administrative Records

We note the importance of testing methods that could expand the use of administrative records for statistical purposes. This research will require cooperation between the Census Bureau and agencies that maintain relevant administrative record systems.

Recommendation 2.2: The Census Bureau should study in the 1995 census test the use of administrative records during nonresponse follow-up as a way to reduce the need for conventional follow-up approaches.

Recommendation 4.3: As part of the 1995 census test, the Census Bureau should construct an administrative records database for the test sites.

Recommendation 4.4: The Census Bureau should establish the testing of record linkage procedures as an important goal of the 1995 census test.

Recommendation 4.5: In preparation for uses of administrative records in the 1995 census test, detailed negotiations between the Census Bureau and the other relevant agencies should begin immediately, with the involvement of the Statistical Policy Office of the Office of Management and Budget (see also Recommendation 4.1).

Address List Development

The construction of an address list is a central element in decennial census operations, and the panel believes the potential benefits are sufficient to justify development, starting in fiscal 1994, and maintenance of a continuously updated address file linked to a geographic database.

Recommendation 1.1: The Census Bureau should continue aggressive development of the TIGER (topologically integrated geographic encoding and referencing) system, the master address file (MAF), and integration of these two systems. TIGER/MAF updating activities should begin in fiscal 1994 and should concentrate first on the sites selected for the 1995 census test.

THE 2000 CENSUS

In addition to recommendations for the 1995 census test, two recommendations refer explicitly to the 2000 census--one proposing a goal for coverage measurement, the other urging consideration of available telephone technology. A third recommendation concerns organizational change to facilitate management of decennial census outreach and promotion.

Recommendation 2.6: Whatever coverage measurement method is used in 2000, the Census Bureau should ensure that a sufficiently large sample is taken so that the single set of counts provides the accuracy needed by data users at pertinent levels of geography.

Recommendation 3.7: The Census Bureau should investigate developing a menu-driven touchtone call routing system for the 2000 census that gives callers to the Census Bureau's toll-free help line quicker access to the specific assistance they want.

Recommendation 3.3: The Census Bureau should assign overall responsibility for decennial census outreach and promotion to a centralized, permanent, and nonpartisan office. The Census Bureau should consider expanding the mission of the extant Public Information Office to include this charge. Evaluation of outreach and promotion programs should be conducted by an independent unit within the Census Bureau.

FURTHER RESEARCH

The remainder of the recommendations endorse topics for further research throughout this decade. This research might inform the 1995 census test, the 2000 census, or census design beyond 2000. These recommendations cover methods for linking records from one or more sources--that is, mail questionnaires, telephone or personal interviews, or administrative data systems--aimed at improving census accuracy by reducing both omissions and erroneous enumerations, the use of sampling and statistical estimation, outreach and promotion, racial and ethnic classification, the long-term use of administrative records, and continuous data collection.

Record Linkage

Recommendation 1.2: The Census Bureau should aggressively pursue its research program on record linkage.

Sampling and Statistical Estimation

Recommendation 2.8: The Census Bureau should vigorously pursue research on statistical estimation now and throughout the decade. Topics should include nonresponse follow-up sampling, coverage estimation, incorporation of varied information sources (including administrative records), indirect estimation for small areas, and matrix sampling.

Recommendation 2.9: The Census Bureau should develop methods for measuring and modeling all sources of error in the census and for showing uncertainty in published tabulations or otherwise enabling users to estimate uncertainty.

Outreach and Promotion

Recommendation 3.4: The Census Bureau should commit the resources necessary to develop and implement customized, local outreach programs to target the traditionally undercounted ethnic minorities. The Census Awareness and Products Program (CAPP) should be expanded and sustained on an ongoing basis, so that it can serve as the primary vehicle for the design and implementation of these outreach programs.

Recommendation 3.6: The Census Bureau should evaluate the use of the Advertising Council to conduct the census media campaign. The Census Bureau should consider the alternatives of working directly with local and regional agencies, undertaking paid media research, and supplementing pro bono advertising with paid advertising in hard-to-enumerate localities.

The Differential Undercount and Racial and Ethnic Classification

Recommendation 3.9: The Census Bureau should conduct further comparative studies of hard-to-enumerate areas, focusing on those parts of the country where three phenomena coincide: a shortage of affordable housing, a high proportion of undocumented immigrants, and the presence of low-income neighborhoods.

Recommendation 3.11: The Census Bureau should consider a major program of research in cognitive anthropology, sociology, and psychology that will comprehensively examine the issue of racial and ethnic identity. This research would contribute to the development of more acceptable racial and ethnic identification questions. In particular, the Census Bureau should consider experimenting with allowing people to select more than one race category in the 1995 census test.

Use of Administrative Records

Recommendation 4.2: The Census Bureau should initiate a systematic process of consultation and research to explore the attitudes of the public, political representatives, and other opinion leaders about the use of administrative records as an integral part of the census. Previous consultations and existing research, such as the yet-to-be-released 1990 Taxpayer Opinion Survey, should be taken into account.

Recommendation 4.6: The Census Bureau should establish a formal program of long-range research and development activities relating to expanded use of administrative records for demographic data.

Continuous Data Collection

Recommendation 5.1: The Census Bureau should continue to explore the feasibility of a continuous measurement component to the 2000 census.

Recommendation 5.2: The Census Bureau should establish a formal set of goals for a continuous measurement program. The Census Bureau should then establish a research plan to determine the extent to which these goals are achievable.

Recommendation 5.3: The Census Bureau should undertake an extensive and systematic evaluation of the benefits from having more frequent census data available for both large and small geographic areas.

Recommendation 5.4: The goals for a continuous measurement program (see Recommendation 5.2) should include phasing in the continuous measurement program during the latter half of the decade prior to the relevant census year.

Recommendation 5.5: As part of its research into the feasibility of and methods for implementing a continuous measurement program, the Census Bureau should undertake a thorough study of the consequences of changes in the instrument over time, as well as changes in mode effects. A plan must be established for incorporating the effects of such changes into the cumulated estimates and into the time series produced by the continuous measurement program.

1

KEY CENSUS DESIGN ISSUES

In some respects, the 1990 U.S. census was the most successful to date. Technological advances in data processing and distribution of data products in CD-ROM (compact disc-read only memory) format have provided census users with unprecedented access and flexibility in handling summary population and housing information. Yet several concerns regarding recent censuses have deepened, and there has been growing momentum and advocacy for fundamental change in census operations.

The two most important concerns are cost and differential coverage. In constant (1990) dollars, the unit costs of counting a household have increased from approximately $10 in 1960, to $20 in 1980, and, to $25 in 1990. Even after adjusting for the decreasing median size of households, census operations have clearly become more expensive. But increases in expenditures have not solved the persistent problem of differential coverage: the Census Bureau estimates that 1.8 percent of the population, or about 4.7 million persons, were not counted in the 1990 census, and the difference in the undercount rates for blacks and nonblacks was 4.4 percentage points, the largest since 1940 (U.S. General Accounting Office, 1992). Differential coverage by race has significant implications for political representation and allocation of federal program funds because these decisions are based on census data at various levels of geography.

These and other issues have drawn the attention not only of the Census Bureau, but also of Congress and other census data users. The Census Bureau has undertaken a research program that reflects a major rethinking of census methodology with the intent of testing design components that represent fundamental change from current census practice.

Early in 1991 the Department of Commerce established a Task Force on the Year 2000 Census to provide an organizational structure for the investigation of issues regarding the 2000 census. The task force comprises a technical committee, a policy committee, and an advisory committee. These committees are concerned with the major issues facing 2000 census planning--particularly, cost and differential coverage.

Our panel is studying feasible methods for the census not only in the year 2000, but also for 2010 and beyond. We have a mandate to make recommendations for features of census design that should be investigated and developed for censuses after the next one. Some features of these future designs could be tested in the near term and further developed in conjunction with the 2000 census, even though they might not be fully implemented until subsequent censuses. Our deliberations lead us to consider all demographic data systems, including current estimates and sample surveys.

The panel has four basic tasks: (1) identify designs to be investigated for the 2000 census; (2) evaluate proposed research on alternative census designs; (3) evaluate the results of the research and the selection of census designs for further consideration, in particular for the series of census tests that begin in 1995; and (4) recommend census designs to be explored for 2010 and succeeding years.

Our emphasis in this interim report on differential undercount and cost has several consequences. First, we give less attention to gross or total census error--that is, omissions plus erroneous enumerations. At several points in the text, we note the importance of the total error concept--for example, when we call for aggressive research on techniques to prevent erroneous, duplicate enumerations during a census with multiple response modes. We believe that census methodology should strive to minimize not only omissions (that produce undercounts) but also erroneous enumerations (that produce overcounts). We expect to give the total error concept further attention in our final report.

Second, our deliberations on cost issues are somewhat muted by the limited amount of information available on the cost-effectiveness of census design components. The Census Bureau has a very detailed cost model (Bureau of the Census, 1992f) for operational planning. This model has been used to estimate costs associated with several designs or design components being considered for the 2000 census, and at the time of this report, work is ongoing on other designs. We look forward to additional information on costs of design options, so that we can expand on the observations contained in this interim report.

Initially, the technical committee of the task force constructed a set of 14 census design alternatives. Each alternative was characterized by one or more unique design components; each was also judged to have the potential to meet the current demands of the decennial census. Six of the 14 designs built on the basic structure of the 1990 census, adding different provisions: multiple ways of responding to the census; varying degrees of sampling and statistical estimation; and targeted methods to overcome barriers to enumeration. Two designs relied entirely or to a very significant extent on administrative records. Four designs would have collected data on fewer topics than have been covered in recent decennial censuses. Two designs proposed collecting census data in two stages or through continuous measurement in the decade following the census year.

The panel's first report to the Census Bureau in December 1992 raised questions about the 14-design approach. Subsequently, the Census Bureau decided to remove its original set of 14 alternative census designs from further consideration. Rather, the 1995 census test will evaluate promising components of the original alternative designs. We strongly support this reorientation of the 2000 census planning process.

Census data collection involves four key steps: (1) the construction of an address frame; (2) an initial process to obtain responses that can be linked to the address frame; (3) a follow-up process to obtain responses from those not covered in the initial process; and (4) a coverage assessment process that estimates the size of the population not covered through the initial and follow-up processes.

The design of a census data collection process in essence amounts to deciding which methods of identification, enumeration, response, and coverage improvement should be applied at each of the steps; whether sampling methods (and the corresponding estimation methods) should be used at any of the four steps; and if sampling methods are used, which methods and at which steps.

The second section of this chapter reviews work done by the Census Bureau as part of its 2000 census research and development program. Subsequent sections discuss some important issues related to the first step of the collection process, the creation of an address frame, and legal and operational issues. We conclude the first chapter with some observations about census planning for the year 2000 and beyond.

Chapter 2 addresses the possible use of sampling and estimation at each stage of the census data collection process, including the question of sampling for content-- that is, methods by which one can forgo the need to ask all census questions of all households. Chapter 3 considers methods with potential for improving response and coverage at various stages of the collection process. Chapter 4 discusses the possible use of administrative records in the four collection steps. Chapter 5 addresses issues related to alternative schemes that would spread the collection of census-type information over a decade, rather than concentrating efforts in a single year.

CENSUS BUREAU EVALUATION CRITERIA AND PROCESS

The Census Bureau developed a set of mandatory and desirable criteria for assessing design alternatives, and it has specified that any design being considered for the 2000 census must satisfy all mandatory criteria. Each design that meets the mandatory criteria will then be assessed according to the set of desirable criteria.

There are six mandatory criteria for the 2000 census design:

(1) not require a constitutional amendment;
(2) meet data needs for reapportionment;
(3) provide data defined by law and past practice for state redistricting;
(4) provide age and race/ethnic data defined by law to meet the requirements of enforcing the Voting Rights Act;
(5) protect the confidentiality of respondents; and,
(6) possess the ability to reduce the differential undercount.

There are 10 desirable criteria for the 2000 census design. Numbers (1) - (5) pertain to the census outcome; (6) - (8) cover the data collection process; and (9) and (10) consider external factors:

(1) result in comparative cost effectiveness with respect to other alternatives under consideration in real terms on a per unit basis;

(2) provide small-area data that the census is uniquely capable of providing;

(3) provide a single, best set of census results produced by legal deadlines for reapportionment and redistricting;

(4) provide an overall high level of coverage;

(5) increase the primary response rate to the census;

(6) reduce the level of respondent burden;

(7) minimize the degree and type of changes needed in federal or state law;

(8) consider the reliance on new or unproven methods or capabilities;

(9) permit full development and testing of its major design features; and,

(10) provide opportunities to involve the U.S. Postal Service, state and local governments, national organizations, and other private, nonprofit, and commercial enterprises.

With regard to the third desirable criterion, the Census Bureau has developed the concept of a "one-number census" that would provide "the best possible single set of results by legal deadlines, . . . based on an appropriate combination of counting, assignment, and statistical techniques" (Miskura, 1993b). In this definition, counting refers to the full array of methods used for direct contact with respondents, including mail questionnaires, personal visits, and telephone calls. Assignment refers to the use of evidence from administrative records to add persons to the count for a specific geographic location without field verification. Statistical techniques for estimation include sampling during follow-up of nonrespondents and procedures for measuring census coverage.

The Census Bureau has expressed its commitment to pursue a one-number census for the year 2000, based on counting, assignment, and estimation. This commitment is reflected in the decision not to test a 1990-style dual-strategy approach in the 1995 census test (Bureau of the Census, 1993f). The specific counting, assignment, and estimation methodologies will be determined by the 2000 census research program. Associated with the one-number census is the principle of integrated coverage measurement, the premise of which is that the three components of a one-number census are designed to complement one another in order to meet legal deadlines. That is, the results from measurement of coverage will be incorporated into the official census results (Miskura, 1993b).

The Census Bureau has also identified eight categories of distinguishing features of a possible 2000 census design. Below, we summarize the Census Bureau's recommendations for testing in 1995 with regard to each feature (Bureau of the Census, 1993e).

Data collection outside the decennial year. The Census Bureau is designing a prototype system for continuous data collection that includes a national "head count" every 10 years. This development work will be carried out in parallel with the 1995 census test that will provide information about accurate and cost-effective methods for the decennial year portion of a continuous measurement program.

Content in the decennial year. The 1995 census test may collect the same content as the 1990 census, although the Census Bureau is considering design options that would involve reduced content in the 1995 test and in the decennial census. Determining the content of the 2000 census will involve ongoing consultation with federal and nonfederal data users and will proceed in parallel with the development of the 2000 census design.

Use of lists. The Census Bureau intends to create and continuously update a master address file that is integrated with its topologically integrated geographic encoding and referencing (TIGER) system database (see Chapter 2). Plans for the 1995 census test call for the list of housing units for the test sites to be developed, at a minimum, with administrative records from the U.S. Postal Service, local records, and available telephone number lists.

Primary response options. For initial contact with respondents, the Census Bureau plans to use mail, face-to-face enumeration, and possibly telephone interviewing, and other electronic modes. To support public response, the Census Bureau plans to include assistance centers, language aids, and, to the maximum extent possible, enumeration at multiple locations (e.g., libraries and shopping malls) as part of the 1995 census test. Administrative records will not be used as a primary method of enumeration, but they will be used for coverage improvement.

Nonresponse follow-up. The Census Bureau recommends continued research on census designs that would either eliminate or substantially shorten the period of time that recent past censuses have allocated to following up nonrespondents to the mail questionnaires. The so-called "truncated" census will be investigated in the 1995 census test if research determines by September 1995 that this design is a viable alternative. The Census Bureau also plans to use, to the extent possible, multiple modes for collecting data during follow-up--in particular, telephone (computer-assisted) interviewing.

Sampling for the count. The Census Bureau recommends testing and evaluation of sampling for nonresponse follow-up during the 1995 census test. Sampling will also be part of the various coverage improvement methods under consideration for testing in 1995. (See Chapter 2 for definitions and discussions of post-enumeration surveys, SuperCensus, and CensusPlus.) The sample census design, which would entail sampling the entire mail-out universe instead of attempting a complete enumeration, has been eliminated from consideration on the grounds that sampling for the count prior to enumeration is unconstitutional.

Sampling for content in the decennial year. The Census Bureau plans to experiment with multiple sample forms (also known as matrix sampling) in the 1995 census test in order to learn how to implement the procedures and produce estimates from this type of sampling.

Statistical estimation. Methods for statistical estimation will be needed in the 1995 census test to support sampling for nonresponse follow-up. Also, statistical estimation will play a central role during the 1995 tests in implementing any of the candidate methods for integrated coverage measurement designed to produce a single set of counts in a one-number census (see Chapter 2).

ADDRESS LISTS AND OTHER RECORDS

Address List Development

Address list development is of central importance to virtually all candidate designs for the 2000 census. Lists containing address information--but without names of residents or other personal data--support several stages of decennial census operations, including distribution of mail questionnaires, follow-up of nonresponding households, and measurement of population coverage. For purposes of coverage improvement, address lists can also be used in conjunction with administrative records that contain information about individuals.

The Census Bureau's 1990 address control file can still serve as a base for the year 2000 master address file, but updating of the 1990 file--that is, processing additions and deletions of housing units, plus other corrections--will have to begin immediately in order to establish a continuously maintained national address list at the Census Bureau in time for the 2000 census. A major initiative for address file updating is included as an item in the fiscal 1994 budget (Scarr, 1993). If this work does not proceed, the Census Bureau will once again have to look to other sources, such as private address lists, in constructing a master list for the decennial census in 2000. In any case, all potential sources of address information--whether governmental or commercial--should be evaluated on their merits.

Work in this area can benefit from increased cooperation with other federal agencies, as well as state and local governments. The Census Bureau is conducting ongoing discussions with the U.S. Postal Service (USPS) regarding options for joint work on address list development. In the 1980 and 1990 censuses, the USPS performed multiple checks on the address list used to mail census questionnaires. During an operation called the advance post office check (APOC), postal carriers checked the census list of housing units on their routes, making corrections and providing information on missing addresses. Evaluations of the effectiveness of APOC and similar address list development operations must consider the accuracy of additional listings--that is, the proportion of duplicate addresses and nonexistent housing units--including any differential performance across geographic areas.

The Census Bureau is also exploring options that would increase involvement of USPS personnel in census operations. One proposal, described in an option paper (Bureau of the Census, 1992c), outlined a cooperative effort that would provide the geographic framework to accept continuous USPS updates of new addresses to the master address file (MAF). The Census Bureau plans to link the MAF with its TIGER system, a digital (computer-readable) map database. The USPS initially expressed interest in the potential value of TIGER in automating more of its mail delivery planning and management activities, but it has judged that more extensive collaboration with the Census Bureau in this endeavor would not be a cost-effective investment. The Census Bureau is exploring the possibility of collaborating with state and local governments on TIGER updating.

Although the USPS has decided against a joint venture on the TIGER system, the USPS and the Census Bureau are pursuing other cooperative efforts in 2000 census planning. A USPS/Census task force has been established, and a subcommittee on rural address conversion is considering how to promote the conversion of rural addresses to a city-style format (Bureau of the Census, 1993b). Both organizations, as well as emergency service providers, could realize potential benefits through address conversion.

The panel believes that a geographic database that is fully integrated with a master address file is a basic requirement for the 2000 census, regardless of the final census design.

> **Recommendation 1.1:** The Census Bureau should continue aggressive development of the TIGER (topologically integrated geographic encoding and referencing) system, the master address file (MAF), and integration of these two systems. TIGER/MAF updating activities should begin in fiscal 1994 and should concentrate first on the sites selected for the 1995 census test.

Successful completion of TIGER/MAF updating for these sites will enable the Census Bureau to gain valuable experience during the 1995 census test.

A continually updated TIGER/MAF system also has tremendous potential for meeting needs for both statistical and nonstatistical uses beyond the decennial census. In its final report, the panel expects to discuss access needs both inside and outside the federal statistical system. TIGER updating is only one aspect of the decennial census that can be viewed in a larger sense as a cooperative venture involving contributions from federal agencies and state and local governments.

Record Linkage

Record linkage is the identification of records belonging to the same unit (e.g., a person or a housing unit) either within a single data set or across two different data sets. For example, the same residence could be listed two different ways in different address records. Multiple listings are more likely to be found in rural areas, where they are a potential source of erroneous enumeration. Needs for record linkage arise when administrative records are used, when multiple response modes are available, and for dual-system estimation as part of any coverage measurement program. Thus, any improvements in the accuracy or efficiency of record linkage will prove valuable for any census design.

Multiple response modes, including special methods for counting hard-to-enumerate populations, constitute a set of methods that could be adapted to many alternative census designs. Work in this area is likely to expand. For example, a recent technology assessment report (Ogden Government Services and IDC Government, 1993) recommended that four home-based technologies be considered for potential use in the 2000 census: (1) telephone; (2) voice recognition; (3) touch-tone data entry with voice recording; and, (4) voice recognition with voice recording.

The Census Bureau has also begun a similar assessment of publicly accessible technologies that would permit response to the census at people's places of work or at public places, such as libraries, post offices, and shopping malls (Bureau of the Census, 1993b).

In considering adoption of multiple response modes, the Census Bureau must address the problem of erroneous enumerations. The 1990 census had approximately 11 million erroneous enumerations (the largest number recorded to date), and unless this problem is controlled, the additional burden posed by multiple responses would seem likely to exacerbate the problem of gross census errors. Toward this end, there may be some value in conducting experimental surveys that gather additional content (e.g., how many different residences, frequency of travel) with the potential to improve the ability to eliminate duplication.

Offering multiple options for responding to the census increases the probability of multiple responses from the same household, thus introducing the possibility of an overcount of those households. To allow maximum use of these multiple-mode techniques, which from a public perception point of view have much to recommend them, the Census Bureau needs to aggressively pursue research on techniques for eliminating duplicate responses so that households with multiple responses are not counted more than once. In fact, limits on the ability to eliminate duplicate records may be the controlling factor with regard to the feasibility of many of the innovations under consideration for the 2000 census design.

Another use of record linkage is for matching records. The Census Bureau conducts ongoing research on record linkage. In conjunction with special censuses of Godfrey, Illinois, and South Tucson, Arizona, work is underway to study the coverage and content of local administrative records and to gain experience with the process of acquiring these files. The Godfrey project involves a postenumeration comparison of voter registration and school district files to the special census. Results of computer and clerical matching indicate that these administrative record systems could add cases to the special census. In addition, clerical matching of tax assessment records suggests that this type of file could be useful in locating multiunit structures (Bureau of the Census, 1993b). The final report from the Godfrey project is scheduled to be released in September 1993. Work on the South Tucson project is ongoing at the time of this report.

> **Recommendation 1.2:** The Census Bureau should aggressively pursue its research program on record linkage.

Record matching and eliminating duplication is important for all three proposed methods for coverage measurement (see Chapter 2). Statistical uses of administrative files, including technical issues in record linkage, are discussed further in Chapter 4.

LEGAL ISSUES

There are many legal issues associated with the decennial census, perhaps the most obvious being the content requirements mandated by the Constitution and by law. The Panel on Census Requirements is conducting a thorough investigation of these content requirements. However, legal issues with possible implications for census methods arise in three contexts: (1) census starting and reporting dates; (2) the use of sampling and statistical estimation; (3) sharing of information from administrative records, including address lists.

April 1 is mandated as the reference census date by Title 13 of the U.S. Code. Title 13 also mandates that the state population counts required for reapportionment be provided 9 months after the census date and that local area data needed for redistricting be provided no later than 12 months after the census date. Thus, the respective deadlines for reapportionment and redistricting data are December 31 of the census year and March 31 of the subsequent year.

There is at least one reason why the April 1 census date should not be considered inviolable. Because moves from one housing unit to another tend to occur at the end and beginning of a month, conducting a census using the first day of the month as the reference date may lead to more frequent errors of misclassification. Canada, for instance, expects gains in accuracy in future censuses by moving its census date to the middle of the month; other countries have had similar experiences.

In weighing alternative methods, concern has been expressed about the ability to provide data by these legislatively mandated deadlines. The panel believes that the need for the December 31 and March 31 deadlines should be reevaluated if using otherwise promising methods would make it unlikely to meet either date. This consideration could apply, for example, to any of the three proposed methods for integrated coverage measurement (see Chapter 2). Promising new methods that can reduce the differential undercount or substantially reduce the costs of the census should not be discarded on grounds of time constraints without further consideration of those legally imposed constraints.

The legal acceptability of using sampling and statistical estimation remains an issue of considerable debate despite supportive rulings in every U.S. District Court case and a similarly favorable position in a recent Congressional Research Service (CRS) report (Lee, 1993). In its interim report (Committee on National Statistics, 1993) the Panel on Census Requirements, relying on reviews by legal scholars, endorsed the CRS position that sampling and statistical estimation are acceptable provided that there has first been a bona fide attempt to count everyone (e.g., by distributing a mail questionnaire). Our recommendations are based on this premise.

Title 39 of the U.S. Code restricts the USPS from disclosing lists of names or addresses, and similar restrictions on the Census Bureau appear in Title 13. Legal considerations thus impose constraints on Census/USPS cooperation. Special temporary legislation was obtained to permit the USPS to share detailed address information with the Census Bureau during the 1984 Address List Compilation Test (Bureau of the Census, 1992e). Similar permanent legislation might provide an opportunity for both agencies to realize significant gains in operational efficiency and consequent cost savings, but any joint activity will need to attend to confidentiality issues regarding the sharing of address lists.

> **Recommendation 1.3:** Congress should enact legislation that permits the sharing of address lists between the Census Bureau and the U.S. Postal Service for the purpose of improving the Census Bureau's master address file.

Chapter 5 contains an expanded, general discussion of legal and technical issues regarding access to content (including address information) from administrative records for statistical purposes.

In its earlier letter report (Committee on National Statistics, 1992), the panel recommended:

> The Census Bureau should seek the cooperation of federal agencies that maintain key administrative record systems, particularly the Internal Revenue Service and the Social Security Administration, in undertaking a series of experimental administrative records minicensuses and related projects, starting as soon as possible and including one concurrent with the 2000 census.

A number of benefits will accrue from improved coordination among federal agencies. Possible examples include work with the Postal Service on address list development and with the Internal Revenue Service and Social Security Administration on statistical use of administrative records. Further interagency cooperation would be essential to the success of a continuous measurement design, for which extensive consultation with other federal agencies would be required to insure that content needs are being met.

OPERATIONAL ISSUES

Uniform Treatment

The legitimacy of the census depends in part on public perception that it fairly treats all geographical areas and demographic groups in the country. "Fair treatment" can be defined in either of two ways: applying the same methods and effort to every area or attaining the same population coverage in every area so that estimates of relative populations of different areas are accurate. These alternatives are in some ways analogous to the competing principles of equality of opportunity and equality of outcome in the provision, for example, of educational services. The proper balance of these principles is a subject of policy debate in provision of services. In the case of the census, however, the priorities are clear: the objective of the census is to measure population accurately, above all to calculate accurate population shares in order to apportion representation properly. Therefore, obtaining equal coverage clearly takes priority over using the same methods in every area. In fact, since experience shows that treating every geographical area and demographic group in the same way leads to differential coverage and therefore to inaccurate population shares, the Census Bureau has a positive duty to use methods designed to close the coverage gap, a duty recognized as a mandatory criterion for any 2000 census candidate design (Bureau of the Census, 1993d).

The approach of developing a targeting model and a "tool kit" of special methods (described further in Chapter 3) is one response to this duty of the Census Bureau. This approach involves constructing a targeting model, based on demographic and housing characteristics, to identify areas at particular risk for low mail return rates or other enumeration problems. These are areas where an accurate enumeration would likely benefit most from the deployment of special techniques drawn from a tool kit of candidate methods--such as using specially trained enumerators or address locators, opening census assistance centers, distributing forms other than by mail, and distributing some forms in languages other than English. These tool-kit methods would be applied as needed in small areas of various sizes. The decision to use any particular tool-kit method would be controlled by some combination of administrative judgment and predictions from the formal targeting model.

The use of administrative records, described in Chapter 4, although not part of the tool kit available to local census offices, might also involve some targeting of efforts to particularly hard-to-enumerate areas or population groups. For example, a list of food stamp recipients could add more names to low-income areas. Other lists, such as state (driver's license) or local government (school registration) lists, would of necessity contribute to the count only in their areas of coverage.

Some critics worry that the use of special methods in certain areas (e.g., tool-kit methods, local administrative records) might make statistical assessments of coverage more difficult or might invalidate assumptions used to combine sample-based estimates and enumeration totals. This criticism must be taken seriously, and the possible effects involved should be evaluated in the 1995 census test and in other ways. Differences in coverage across areas or groups can be corrected by appropriate use of coverage measurement and population estimation (see Chapter 2). The concern is that special tool-kit methods or local administrative records would be used differentially, and this concern should be addressed.

For example, suppose black renters in central cities correspond to a cell (or a poststratum) in an estimation method similar to the 1990 Post-Enumeration Survey (PES), used now for coverage measurement and estimation. Suppose further that special tool-kit methods were used for "renters in central cities" (or for "black renters in central cities"). In the case where the "treatment" of applying a tool-kit method corresponds to a poststratum, or where a poststratum can be defined on the basis of tool-kit use, the estimation procedure could correct for undercoverage of this group without making extra assumptions. If tool-kit methods improve the coverage of a given group recognized as a poststratum, then the statistical estimation of coverage will detect higher levels of coverage. This case assumes that the use of tool-kit methods does not affect the dependence between enumeration (census capture) and catchability in the samples used to estimate coverage. We therefore believe that the use of special methods--those from the tool kit--or local administrative records for a group or area already defined as a poststratum in the estimation procedure does not create any new statistical problems. Good initial coverage through enumeration and assignment is still very desirable, because with high levels of initial coverage final estimates are less dependent on estimation and variance (or mean-squared error) is reduced.

A more serious concern arises if different enumeration methods (e.g., special tool-kit methods) are applied *within* an area corresponding to an estimation cell or poststratum. For example, suppose that local administrative records or special tool kits are applied to a particular political subdivision within a poststratum cell, but not to the entire poststratum or cell. In this case, it might be difficult to assess the possible biases in estimation that might be created by differential application of tool-kit methods if the methods alter the dependence between enumeration odds and sample catchability. Similar problems might arise if truncation of nonresponse follow-up (i.e., the date on which follow-up of mail respondents is stopped) differs among district offices, as has been the case in past censuses. Cell-based estimation methods applied as in the past will not take account of differentials within poststratum cells.

Several points should be considered in defense of census procedures that treat different areas differently. First, with any practical poststratification scheme (cell definition), there will be differences among areas within the cell, both in the underlying conditions affecting census coverage and in the conduct of the census. This has always been the case: for example, mail return rates and district office closeout dates varied substantially in the 1990 census. Furthermore, these differences exist regardless of whether or not estimation is part of the census methodology. Second, differences in treatment can be justified by local differences in conditions, especially if the decision to use a special method is determined by an objective decision procedure. If decisions are based on knowledge about the distribution of hard-to-count populations, such differences in treatment will tend to reduce differentials in outcome. Third, differences in treatment based on difficulty of enumeration or on the usefulness of particular techniques in different areas are probably more justifiable than those that result from haphazard implementation of coverage improvement programs or the assertiveness and technical capabilities of local authorities.

However, certain practices may arouse suspicion and be difficult to defend. By systematically planning the use of special methods with a view to a defensible standard of uniformity, charges of arbitrariness can be defended. If special enumeration methods are targeted to certain areas but not to others with similar characteristics, their application will appear to be arbitrary. The same will be true if they are targeted toward only some ethnic or socioeconomic groups but not to others with similar undercoverage problems. Systematic and complete planning for use of these methods, based on objective criteria, can defend against the appearance of arbitrariness.

The use of administrative records that are only available in some areas, or that are of drastically varying quality in different areas, may create an appearance of unfairness. By making as much use as possible of record systems with national coverage or at least some degree of national uniformity, the perception of unfairness can be avoided. Alternatively, administrative records could be consistently used for undercovered groups, such as for food stamp recipients, as noted above. Inevitably, there will be different levels of success in operations of various district offices due to varying local conditions. By considering in advance rules for closeout of district office operations and for distribution of additional resources to district offices--rules that are designed to optimize uniformity of coverage within the constraints of varying conditions--the Census Bureau will be best able to defend its decisions. Of course, as in past censuses, the actual degree of uniformity attained will be limited by practical constraints.

Paradoxically, the Census Bureau's improved capabilities and success in tracking census operations, together with growing knowledge and awareness about factors that may affect differential undercount, create a climate in which even more than usual care must be given to avoid any appearance of arbitrariness or favoritism.

Residence Rules

Residence rules and their application are important for a number of reasons. First, it is important to have consistent rules so that each person is counted in only one place (especially when matching records or eliminating duplication from multiple information sources is done). Second, people should be assigned to the correct location, as defined by the residence rules in effect. Third, people should not be excluded solely because the residence rules do not easily apply to them.

The Census Bureau has conducted the census on the basis of *de jure* rather than *de facto* residence--that is, people are essentially asked "Where were you usually resident on census day?" rather than "Where did you actually stay on census day?" The *de jure* approach has the advantage of defining residency in a way that does not depend on what happened on a particular day, but it can create difficulties for people whose *de jure* residency is hard to determine or who have none at all, such as homeless people and young people who move about from place to place. Although residency is ultimately defined by the wording of the questionnaire, consideration should be given to making the definitions work for as many people as possible.

(The concept of residency reappears at various points in subsequent chapters. Residence rules are discussed further, and recommendations are offered in Chapter 3, particularly with regard to improving within-household coverage and handling complicated living situations. That chapter also considers ideas for collecting a "census night" roster followed by questions to assign *de jure* residence.)

Attention must be given to defining residency consistently throughout all stages of census operations: questionnaire mailing and questionnaire return and subsequent nonresponse follow-up and coverage measurement activities. This is particularly critical for coverage measurement programs, such as CensusPlus and the postenumeration survey (see Chapter 2), since they must determine census-day residency weeks or months after the fact. Administrative records have different definitions of residency, both because of the different purposes and laws under which they are collected and because some are continuously updated while others follow set time schedules. Use of administrative records will require ways of reconciling these differences (see Chapter 4).

Continuous Infrastructure

Common sense, complemented by anecdotal evidence, suggests several benefits associated with the Census Bureau's maintaining a continuous presence in local areas throughout the decade. Ongoing activities could contribute to more effective outreach and promotion, thus improving public response and decreasing costs associated with nonresponse follow-up. This theme is explored more fully in Chapter 3. Also, organizational efficiencies might be realized by reducing the amount of temporary staff needed in the 10-year census cycle. The potential benefits could be especially significant if a continuous measurement program is adopted. Chapter 5 assesses the pros and cons of a continuous measurement census design. The Census Bureau is planning to continue work to develop this option in parallel with the 1995 census test.

PLANNING FOR THE 2000 AND FUTURE CENSUSES

The 1995 census test is of critical importance to the goal of an improved and more efficient census in the year 2000. Because of the extensive operational planning that must occur prior to 2000, the 1995 test represents the major opportunity to investigate fundamental reform without jeopardizing the integrity of the 2000 census. It is essential that adequate resources are invested in planning and executing this mid-decade test. Otherwise, the 2000 census will have a design very similar to that of the 1990 census, with the risk of continually rising unit costs, or an inadequately tested design that risks lost demographic information and population counts of unknown or inferior quality.

The 1995 census test should be structured to provide specific information to answer a limited and well-defined set of questions about alternative census methods. To the extent feasible, statistical designs such as fractional factorial experiments should be carried out, although the panel recognizes that operational issues will limit the scientific complexity of the 1995 census test. In particular, the test should include evaluation components that provide a basis for assessing cost-effectiveness.

The operational constraints on the 1995 census test underscore the importance of learning as much as possible from other research. For example, simulation studies using 1990 census data can investigate the effects of truncating nonresponse follow-up operations at different points in time, using different rates of sampling nonrespondents for follow-up, and applying different coverage measurement methods. Similarly, not all methods need to be tested in large-scale field settings. To ease experimental complexity, certain methods might be excluded from large-scale field testing in 1995 when such an exclusion would not disrupt the research and development program or where smaller experiments conducted simultaneously with the 1995 census test will provide useful information.

The panel's letter report (Committee on National Statistics, 1992) included the following two recommendations:

The Census Bureau should initiate a separate program of research on administrative records, focusing primarily on the 2010 census and on current estimates programs. The research program should be funded separately from the 2000 census research and development activities, but there should be close liaison between them.

The Census Bureau should undertake a planning study, in collaboration with other agencies and contract support as needed, that would develop one or more detailed design options for a 2010 administrative records census. The study would have two major goals: to identify the steps that would need to be taken, early in this decade, to make a 2010 administrative records census possible and to set the stage for a national debate on the desirability of an administrative records census. The study, or at least its initial phases, should be completed during the current fiscal year.

The Census Bureau has indicated that it is giving serious consideration to submitting a budget initiative to form a long-term census research staff in fiscal 1995. Such an action is compatible with the above recommendations. However, we caution that the budget for a long-term staff should be independent of the funding cycle for short-term research and development work on the next decennial census (see Bradburn, 1993). The year 2000 research and development staff is scheduled to be disbanded at the end of 1995, yet personnel will be needed to evaluate the results of the 1995 census test. Consideration should be given to revising organizational structures to minimize the extent to which short-term and long-term research divisions would compete for personnel and other resources. (Chapter 4 includes a discussion of the long-term research that is needed to develop new, potentially cost-effective uses of administrative records for statistical purposes in the decennial census and other demographic programs.)

2

SAMPLING AND STATISTICAL ESTIMATION

This chapter focuses on uses of sampling and statistical estimation for improving the 2000 census. These techniques are particularly relevant for achieving two main goals of 2000 census research and development: reducing differential coverage and controlling operational costs.

Although the Census Bureau has ruled out a sample census for 2000, several uses of sampling are being considered:

(1) Sampling households that do not respond to the census mailing could substantially reduce the cost of nonresponse follow-up. (Because of its close interaction with sampling for nonresponse follow-up, we also discuss truncation of the nonresponse follow-up period.)

(2) Any coverage measurement program designed to reduce the differential undercount would require sampling. Each of the three coverage measurement methods under consideration would involve field operations in a sample of blocks.

(3) Sampling for content is also very likely in 2000--involving either a single long form assigned to a sample of households, as in 1990, or multiple sample forms (matrix sampling).

The three major sections of this chapter discuss these topics in turn.

The use of sampling necessarily entails the use of statistical estimation as well, because information from sampled units must be used to generate estimates for units omitted from the sample. The nature of these methods is partly, but not entirely, determined by the type of sampling performed. (Statistical estimation is discussed in the last section of the chapter.)

In addition to the obvious relationships between sampling and statistical estimation, the various uses of sampling interact in important ways. Thus, decisions about any of the particular aspects should not be made without attention to the others. For example, truncation or sampling of nonresponse follow-up could affect coverage measurement in terms of the sample size required, the resources available, and the schedule for implementation.

NONRESPONSE FOLLOW-UP

Nonresponse follow-up was a very costly and troublesome part of the 1990 census. The Census Bureau estimates that nonresponse follow-up operations cost approximately $378 million in direct costs, 15 percent of the $2.6 billion 10-year cost of the census (Bureau of the Census, 1992f). Field follow-up activities--consisting mainly of rechecking housing units initially reported as vacant or nonexistent in nonresponse follow-up operations--cost an additional $115 million.[1] Each 1 percent of nonresponse to the mailed questionnaire is estimated to have added approximately $17 million to the cost of the census.

Perhaps just as important, nonresponse follow-up took much longer than anticipated in some sites (particularly, New York City), pushing back the schedule for completion of the census and therefore for the Post-Enumeration Survey (PES) as well. Even without delays in schedule, the latter stages of census operations typically suffer degradation of data quality. Ericksen et al. (1991) report that, for the 1990 census, the rate of erroneous enumeration on mailout-mailback was 3.1 percent. On nonresponse follow-up, the rate was 11.3 percent; on field follow-up, the rate was 19.4 percent.

Much of the problem in 1990 resulted from mailback response rates that were lower than expected. Item nonresponse also contributed to the follow-up work because additional contacts are required to complete missing items. A variety of response improvement programs can be expected to improve mailback rates and, perhaps, to speed nonresponse follow-up operations. Even so, a 1990-style nonresponse follow-up operation is sure to be very expensive. Thus, methods that reduce the scope of nonresponse follow-up without undue sacrifices in the accuracy of the count or the content deserve serious consideration for the year 2000.

Major Nonresponse Follow-Up Innovations

The Census Bureau is considering three main techniques that would greatly reduce the cost of nonresponse follow-up: truncation, shortening the time period for field operations; sampling, carrying out nonresponse follow-up operations for a sample of households or blocks; and use of administrative records to replace some of the field data collection.

Simple truncation of nonresponse follow-up means stopping nonresponse follow-up operations in all areas at an earlier date than in a 1990-style census. The operations would be curtailed either at a predetermined time or when some predetermined percentage of nonresponse cases had been resolved. A range of truncation dates have been considered in the Census Bureau's research on this topic,

---

[1]The U.S. General Accounting Office (1992) estimates for nonresponse follow-up in the 1990 census are virtually the same: approximately $560 million, including $377 million in direct costs and $183 million in indirect costs; the total cost of field follow-up was estimated at $170 million, including approximately $56 million in indirect costs.

including April 21 (at the beginning of nonresponse follow-up operations, 3 weeks after census day), June 2 (after 6 weeks of nonresponse follow-up), and June 30 (near the end of nonresponse follow-up work). Of the population included in the final census total, the Census Bureau counted approximately 70 percent, 90 percent, and 98 percent, respectively, by these dates in 1990.

Sampling for nonresponse follow-up implies that enumerators would follow up only a sample of mailout addresses for which a mail form had not been returned. Current research at the Census Bureau is considering using either the individual address or the block as the sampling unit. If responses from mailback nonrespondents are correlated within blocks, then sampling by blocks would increase the variance of block-level population estimates relative to those derived from a sample of housing units. However, sampling by blocks appears to offer three advantages that might make it preferable. First, it seems likely that only block sampling would permit adding persons who do not correspond to an original address. Second, potential cost savings in field operations might accrue from block clustering. Third, coverage measurement methods that compare their own enumeration to the regular census enumeration in the same blocks would work much better in blocks, where all nonresponding households are followed up (see descriptions of CensusPlus and PES in the next section).

Sampling and truncation may also play a role in controlling costs associated with follow-up for item nonresponse, although the design issues are somewhat different than those for unit nonresponse, and the design need not be the same. Truncation of this aspect of follow-up may control costs and speed completion of the follow-up operation. Sampling may be useful by providing information that can be used to impute missing items for nonsampled units. Costs per household for completing missing items for responding households by telephone interview are certainly lower than those for completing full forms for nonresponding households. Yet there is potentially much more information available to guide item imputation (from completed items for the same household or from external sources such as administrative records) than there is for imputing a whole nonresponding household. As McKenney and Cresce (1992) note, decisions on follow-up procedures can have a substantial effect on the amount of information that must be allocated by models versus the amount that is obtained by telephone or field follow-up.

Pros and Cons of the Innovations

Both truncation and sampling offer the opportunity for substantial cost savings of hundreds of millions of dollars, in part by shortening the time of the nonresponse follow-up period. Compressing nonresponse follow-up offers several benefits. Two of the coverage measurement methods under consideration for the 2000 census, CensusPlus and PES, would benefit from starting earlier because fewer people would have moved between April 1 and the time of the coverage measurement operation, and there would be more time for data processing and analysis before counts were due. These considerations have implications for a truncated nonresponse follow-up because the full benefits of accelerating census schedules would only be obtained if coverage improvement programs (such as the recheck of vacant housing units) were also truncated, so that CensusPlus or PES operations commenced at an early date. Sampling might also improve the accuracy of the nonresponse follow-up operation because the reduction in workload could permit hiring more qualified personnel with smaller caseloads, resulting in earlier contact attempts and lower incidences of moving between April 1 and contact time.

In contrast to these cost and operational advantages, both truncation and sampling have negative implications for the precision of small-area enumeration. Truncation of nonresponse follow-up could be expected to increase both the undercount and differential coverage of regular census enumeration. That result would increase the coverage measurement sample size necessary to achieve the same degree of precision in the final one-number census population totals that would be achieved in conjunction with a full nonresponse follow-up operation. Simple truncation would also adversely affect the quality of long-form data by creating nonresponse bias with no obvious method for correction.

Sampling for nonresponse follow-up would have somewhat different consequences on the precision of counts. If block sampling is used and coverage measurement is done in a subsample of those blocks, there would not be a direct increase in the size requirements for the coverage measurement sample. However, the precision of block-level counts for nonsample blocks would suffer due to the need for indirect estimation of all mailout nonrespondents in those blocks. At 1990 mail response rates, estimation would be required to complete about 30 percent of the population for those blocks, rather than the 1.5 percent or so that would be added for undercount in blocks with complete nonresponse follow-up. Two points are relevant to this discussion. First, count estimates requiring imputation for nonresponse before nonresponse follow-up would contain more error that estimates based on 1990-type nonresponse follow-up. Second, the additional error would also appear in counts for aggregations of blocks.

Two-Stage Nonresponse Follow-Up

Although both truncation and sampling have merit on their own, they may work even better in combination. A two-stage nonresponse follow-up operation would consist of a truncated first stage carried out in 100 percent of blocks--which would try to quickly resolve a substantial fraction of cases using some combination of telephone interviews, field work, and assignment from administrative records--followed by extended nonresponse follow-up in a sample of blocks.

A combination could bring together some of the best features of each strategy. The fraction of the population that would have to be estimated indirectly would be smaller than with a single-stage sample nonresponse follow-up strategy, because the status of many of the nonresponding addresses could be resolved in a brief first-stage follow-up (of perhaps 2 or 3 weeks); therefore, uncertainties due to sampling and estimation would be smaller as well. At the same time, the sample at the second stage of nonresponse follow-up would be sufficiently dense to capture local variations in response rates, and follow-up operations and could make use of the most skilled of the enumerators from the first-stage operation. This would mitigate one of the potential defects of truncation: that local variations in mailback response and nonresponse follow-up operations are so large that differential coverage cannot be measured with acceptable precision by the coverage measurement survey. We recognize, however, that a combined strategy may limit cost savings in comparison with a single-stage approach because of inefficiencies in administration and staffing. Both the statistical properties of a two-stage nonresponse follow-up and the operational costs and benefits in terms of quality and staffing costs require further investigation. We note that the final report of a previous National Research Council panel (Citro and Cohen, 1985:27) also considered the merits of combining truncation with sampling for nonresponse follow-up:

> Recommendation 6.2. We recommend that the Census Bureau include the testing of sampling in follow-up as part of the 1987 pretest program. We recommend that in its research the Census Bureau emphasize tests of sampling for the later stages of follow-up.

Nonresponse follow-up truncation, sampling, or a combination of the two would affect accuracy of counts and of content. These effects would be most noticeable at the small-area levels. The loss of precision for counts relative to a full nonresponse follow-up (no sampling, truncation at a relatively late date) would depend on details of the design, including the length of follow-up before truncation, the rate for posttruncation follow-up, if any, and sampling rates in the coverage measurement survey. In addition, the loss of precision, and therefore the eventual choice of designs, would depend on the availability of supplementary information, the amount of local variation in response and coverage rates, and the appropriateness of estimation procedures. The tradeoff between cost and variance, at various levels of geographical detail, is an important aspect of nonresponse follow-up design that could be investigated with a combination of algebraic models and simulations using 1990 data.

We endorse the recent recommendations of the Panel on Census Requirements (Committee on National Statistics, 1993) that sampling for nonresponse follow-up be investigated in the 1995 census test. In addition, we suggest specific topics for consideration during research and evaluation.

> **Recommendation 2.1:** The Census Bureau should continue research on nonresponse follow-up sampling and truncation, including consideration of a combined strategy with a truncated first stage and sampling during a second stage of follow-up. Evaluation should consider effects of the nonresponse follow-up design on costs and on variance at a variety of geographic levels,

from states to small areas.

Use of Administrative Records During Nonresponse Follow-Up

Administrative records may play an important role in making nonresponse follow-up more efficient. Possible uses of administrative records include the following:

(1) to support nonresponse follow-up by facilitating identification of residents of nonresponding addresses and making it easier to reach them by telephone;

(2) to complete information for nonresponding addresses, if an administrative record that can be identified with that address is sufficiently complete and reliable;

(3) to complete missing items for responding households, using information in the completed items to verify that the administrative record and the census questionnaire refer to the same household; and

(4) as background information to make possible more accurate estimation of persons in nonsample blocks with a sampled nonresponse follow-up.

If these uses prove effective, they could dramatically shorten the period needed for adequate truncated nonresponse follow-up or for the first stage in a two-stage nonresponse follow-up. (Administrative records have similar uses with regard to coverage measurement; see Chapter 4.)

Recommendation 2.2: The Census Bureau should study in the 1995 census test the use of administrative records during nonresponse follow-up as a way to reduce the need for conventional follow-up approaches.

COVERAGE MEASUREMENT METHODS

Previous Coverage Measurement Programs

The Census Bureau has attempted to systematically measure coverage of the census since 1950 (Coale, 1955; Himes and Clogg, 1992). The 1980 Post-Enumeration Program was designed as an evaluation program for the 1980 census. Following that census, a number of states, local governments, and other plaintiffs sued to have the Census Bureau adjust population totals for differential undercoverage. Several lawsuits were filed, of which two went to trial. In one of these, the New York case, the judge in December 1987 ruled against the plaintiffs.

The 1990 Post-Enumeration Survey (PES) was designed to measure undercoverage and overcoverage, with a view to adjusting for undercount if the PES was found to support sufficiently credible, precise, and reliable population estimates. The PES was designed as two surveys based on identical samples of 5,000 block clusters, one to measure undercoverage and one to measure erroneous enumerations in the census. The fundamental statistical assumption of the PES methodology is independence between capture in the census and in the PES, conditional on adjustment cell or poststratum. The 1990 PES has been extensively documented (Hogan, 1992, 1993; Mulry and Spencer, 1991).

After a period of intensive evaluation, the Census Bureau recommended adjustment of the 1990 census, but the Secretary of Commerce did not accept the recommendation. In one of several lawsuits filed after the 1990 census, the presiding judge observed that "Plaintiffs have made a powerful case that discretion would have been more wisely employed in favor of adjustment...," but he also found that the Secretary's decision was not "arbitrary or capricious" and ruled that, therefore, the decision could stand (see McLaughlin, 1993).

The Census Bureau's coverage evaluation efforts have demonstrated that certain groups are systematically undercounted relative to the rest of the population. Although response improvement programs--such as questionnaire simplification and reminder postcards--show promise for improving the mailback rate compared with 1990, early tests (see Chapter 3) suggest that they will have little effect, if any, on differential coverage. Other programs targeted at improving coverage of hard-to-reach populations may help to reduce differential coverage (see Chapter 3), but past experience suggests that they are unlikely to close the gap, especially at acceptable cost levels. For example, during the 1990 census, the recheck of vacant or nonexistent housing units added about 1.5 million persons, but over 30 percent of the additions were subsequently estimated to be erroneous. Similarly, the parolee-probationer check added between 400,000 and 500,000 persons to the final census counts, but about half of those persons were later estimated to have been enumerated erroneously (U.S. General Accounting Office, 1992; see Citro and Cohen, 1985:Ch. 5, for additional discussion of coverage improvement programs).

The One-Number Census

Current plans for the 2000 census are predicated on a strategy of integrated coverage measurement leading to a one-number census. In this approach, coverage measurement and statistical estimation are integrated into census methodology, rather than being regarded as separate operations that might be used to adjust the census. A one-number census offers several advantages over the dual strategy that was adopted for the 1990 census. First, it allows for the most cost-effective design because it permits planning cost and quality improvements in the census, particularly with regard to closing the differential coverage gap, that coverage measurement makes possible. Second, decisions about whether to implement response improvement programs aimed at special populations can be made on the basis of improving accuracy rather than on the basis of which groups would be helped or hurt. If the decision to use estimation and the basic estimation strategy (although not necessarily all the details of the procedure) are specified at the beginning of the census process, concerns that decisions have been influenced by a desire to benefit certain geographic or demographic groups will be forestalled. Finally, a one-number census that enjoys the support of the scientific community will have greater credibility with the American public. At the same time, it requires that there be sufficient confidence in the success of the coverage measurement aspect of the program to proceed with plans based on it. We believe that the Census Bureau's experience with the Post-Enumeration Survey in 1990 indicates that a coverage measurement method can be designed that would reduce differential coverage in the 2000 census (Mulry and Spencer, 1993; Bureau of the Census, 1992b).

We argue above that reduction of census costs and reduction of differentials in coverage cannot occur simultaneously without coverage measurement and the use of statistical estimation. In this section, we argue that the strategy of integrated coverage measurement possesses several important advantages over the dual-strategy approach that was adopted for the 1990 census. Together, these arguments lead us to an endorsement of the Census Bureau's position regarding coverage measurement for the 2000 census.

> **Recommendation 2.3:** We endorse the Census Bureau's stated goal of achieving a one-number census in 2000 that incorporates the results from coverage measurement programs, including programs involving sampling and statistical estimation, into the official census population totals. We recommend that research on alternative methodologies continue in pursuit of this goal.

Alternative Coverage Measurement Methods

The Census Bureau has identified three candidate methods for coverage measurement: the PES (at least conceptually similar to the 1990 methodology) and two new methods, CensusPlus and SuperCensus (Bureau of the Census, 1993e).

The Post-Enumeration Survey (PES) is an independent survey conducted after the census in a sample of blocks for the purpose of measuring census coverage. The respondents are matched to the original enumeration on a case-by-case basis. Statistical methods for ratio estimation can then be applied to obtain an estimate of the population size. The Census Bureau's PES methodology involves two overlapping sample surveys: a sample of census enumerations that measures erroneous census enumerations (the E sample) and a sample of the population that measures census omissions (the P sample) (see Mulry, 1992).

CensusPlus selects a sample of blocks and, using the census enumeration as a starting point, continues enumeration efforts in these blocks after the regular census is completed in an attempt to achieve a complete count. The count is improved by using special methods--such as administrative lists and highly trained interviewers--that are too expensive to use everywhere. The additional enumerations in the CensusPlus sample areas are used to develop population estimates for the nonsample areas by using statistical methods, such as ratio estimation (Mulry, 1992).

SuperCensus also selects a sample of blocks and conducts the enumeration with special methods similar to those described in CensusPlus. Like CensusPlus, SuperCensus attempts to conduct a complete census in the sampled blocks. The key difference is that no regular census takes place in these blocks: SuperCensus operations begin at the same time as, or even earlier than, the census in other blocks. This timing avoids most of the problems faced by PES or CensusPlus for people who move in the months following census day. Population estimates are based on applying the ratio of people to housing units observed in the sample blocks--or some other measure that is available for every block prior to the census--to the total number of housing units (Mulry, 1992).

The distinguishing feature of the PES is that the coverage measurement survey takes place after the basic census enumeration and is intended to be operationally and statistically independent of that enumeration. The PES methodology has no necessary connection to other features of the 1990 coverage measurement effort, such as the use of a dual strategy in which separate adjusted and unadjusted counts were calculated and the choice between them was made after the fact.

CensusPlus, like the PES, takes place after the basic census enumeration. Coverage estimation for CensusPlus involves techniques similar to those for the PES. For both coverage measurement methods, the ratio used in estimation is the correct population total to the census enumeration for that block. The key difference between CensusPlus and PES is that CensusPlus does not require independence between the basic enumeration and coverage measurement operations. This characteristic allows CensusPlus to use and build on the information collected during the regular census operations. However, the independence requirement is replaced by one of complete coverage by CensusPlus in sample blocks.

At the time of this report, the CensusPlus and SuperCensus methods for coverage measurement are not mature designs. Work is needed to define these options more fully so that they can be subjected to simulation studies, field testing, and comparative evaluation against the post-enumeration survey.

Selection Criteria

Four criteria are critical to selection of a coverage measurement methodology for the 2000 census:

(1) *Acceptable degree of bias*. In practice, no coverage measurement method will completely eliminate differential coverage. However, the bias should be substantially smaller than the differential coverage that the method is intended to correct.

(2) *Adequate precision of population estimates for various levels of geography achievable at a fixed cost*. Of course, the actual variance is determined by the size of the coverage measurement budget and the resulting sample size.

(3) *Operational and scheduling feasibility*. The method needs to be

operationally feasible and able to meet reporting deadlines (see Chapter 1).

(4) *Ability to demonstrate that the method meets the other criteria.* In practice, this means that there must be a satisfactory methodology for evaluating the chosen coverage measurement methodology, in tests as well as during the census. This is especially important for the assumptions that determine whether the coverage estimates will be biased.

We have identified specific major hurdles that apply to the three major contenders for alternative coverage measurement methods. For the PES, there are three: (1) the assumption of independence, conditional on poststratification variables, between inclusion in the census and the PES samples, (2) the need for accurate matching of names reported in the census and PES, and (3) the ability to meet reporting deadlines (after the extensive matching and verification operations).

For CensusPlus, there are five major hurdles: (1) the ability to obtain complete coverage (i.e., find everyone by the end of CensusPlus), (2) the ability to eliminate duplication of names in order to avoid overcounting during CensusPlus, (3) resolving place- of-residence problems (see Chapter 1), (4) development of a way to estimate the number of erroneous enumerations that occurred during the regular census, and (5) the ability to meet reporting deadlines (probably less of a concern than for the PES, because CensusPlus would build on census enumerations, while the PES starts anew).

For SuperCensus, there are four major hurdles: (1) the ability to obtain complete coverage (i.e., find everyone by the end of SuperCensus), (2) the ability to eliminate duplicated names in order to avoid overcounting during SuperCensus, (3) resolving place-of-residence problems, and (4) achieving sufficient accuracy within reasonable cost limits. There is reason to believe the last hurdle is particularly severe for the SuperCensus approach. The SuperCensus would require estimating ratios of person counts (e.g., black males aged 18-24) to housing unit counts. The variance of one of these estimated ratios is roughly proportional to the between-block variance of the ratio, and the Census Bureau's research on a sample census (Isaki et al., 1993) seems to indicate high between-block variation in these ratios. Therefore, SuperCensus may require a much larger sample size than CensusPlus or PES to achieve the same level of precision. It should be possible to resolve this issue, at least preliminarily, using 1990 PES counts (or regular census counts) to simulate a sample of SuperCensus blocks.

> **Recommendation 2.4:** Before final design of the 1995 census test, the Census Bureau should critically evaluate the SuperCensus method of coverage measurement by using 1990 data to learn whether adequately precise coverage estimates are possible using ratios to the housing base.

As noted in Chapter 1, definitions of residency in a particular location are an issue for every coverage measurement method, complicated by people who move shortly after the census or whose residency is transient around census day. The nature of the issue, however, differs somewhat among methods. With the PES, it is only necessary to determine whether persons located in the PES were enumerated in the census anywhere, or in practice, within some search area determined by the practicalities of the search operation. With CensusPlus it would be necessary to determine which of the persons found in the survey several months later were resident in sample blocks on census day according to census rules, and conversely, to achieve near-complete coverage of those persons who were resident in the sample blocks. Finally, SuperCensus, like CensusPlus, would have to locate and geographically assign all persons, and only those persons, who were officially resident in sample blocks on census day. However, because SuperCensus would be carried out on an earlier schedule than CensusPlus, it might be somewhat easier to deal with place of residency.

Development and Testing

The Census Bureau has correctly identified that either of the new coverage measurement methods would require more research and development than would the PES if it is to become the method used in 2000. However, we are concerned by the description of the PES approach ". . . partly as a fallback position in the event the SuperCensus/CensusPlus approach does not prove viable based on our research or on results of the 1995 Census Test" (Bureau of the Census, 1993d:24). Because both CensusPlus and SuperCensus involve an assumption of near-complete coverage that has not been demonstrated by any census method to date, the importance of maintaining the PES as a tested alternative should not be minimized.

We are concerned that exclusion of the PES from the 1995 census test will jeopardize its status as a candidate method for coverage measurement in the 2000 census. Because the PES is the method that is best supported by past experience, we believe it should be tested in combination with new features that will be tried in 1995, possibly including integrated coverage measurement, multiple response modes, and nonresponse follow-up truncation. In particular, the timeliness of the PES as part of an integrated coverage measurement strategy can only be demonstrated in a census test environment. Even if SuperCensus or CensusPlus proves possible on the basis of testing in 1995, the PES may still be the best choice. However, unless a fair, comparative evaluation of all candidate methods is undertaken, it may be difficult to justify choosing the PES over a method tested in 1995.

> **Recommendation 2.5:** Development and testing of methodology for the Post-Enumeration Survey (PES) should continue in parallel with other methods until another method proves superior in operational tests. All methods still under consideration--including the PES--should be evaluated critically against common criteria.

Note that the selection criteria outlined in the preceding section may be commonly applied to all candidate methods--that is, the criteria are independent of any particular feature of the candidate methods. To produce the information required, coverage measurement will need to be tested in a substantial proportion of the 1995 census test blocks. We note that this will also provide valuable information about the success of response improvement programs in reducing differential coverage.

Interaction between coverage measurement and other design features needs to be studied. The best choice of coverage measurement method may depend on other factors in the 2000 census. For example, we believe that speeding up nonresponse follow-up may improve the accuracy of the PES and CensusPlus. Thus, it would be valuable to learn about the interaction between coverage measurement methodology and nonresponse follow-up design, including truncation date and the use of sampling.

Coverage Measurement Sample in the 2000 Census

We anticipate that estimates that meet the demands of integrated coverage measurement in the year 2000 will require a much larger sample size than that used in the 1990 PES, although the precise determination of this size will depend on the coverage measurement and estimation methods used. The precision of coverage measurement depends critically on sample size and the poststratification design (choice of adjustment cells). For a given sample size, if adjustment cells are too large, they will fail to capture important heterogeneity in census coverage rates, which will affect the accuracy of corrections for small areas. The issue of heterogeneity within adjustment cells was cited as an argument against adjustment of the population base for intercensal estimates (Bryant, 1993). If adjustment cells are too small, there will be inadequate sample size to obtain estimates of acceptable precision, although modeling may be of some assistance in this situation; again, the accuracy of estimates for small areas will be most affected. Only with adequate sample size can both of these problems be mitigated. This sample size calculation should be based on analysis of data from the 1990 census and the 1995 census test.

Coverage measurement sample size also interacts with other features discussed in this chapter, including truncation or nonresponse follow-up sampling: there is a tradeoff between cost savings through these methods and a corresponding requirement for expansion of the coverage measurement sample in order to obtain sufficiently precise estimates of the larger undercoverage that would result. These tradeoffs may favor increasing the size of coverage measurement relative to nonresponse follow-up. The cost of the PES, $50-60 million in 1990, was small relative to that of nonresponse follow-up. In addition to cost considerations, it would be important to demonstrate that field management and data processing operations for a larger coverage measurement program could be administered.

Recommendation 2.6: Whatever coverage measurement method is used in 2000, the Census Bureau should ensure that a sufficiently large sample is taken so that the single set of counts provides the accuracy needed by data users at pertinent levels of geography.

SAMPLING FOR CONTENT: MATRIX SAMPLING

Census methodology has involved sampling for content since 1940. In recent censuses, sampling for content has been accomplished through the use of short and long forms. The long form has been distributed to a sample of households, with the sampling rate depending on the type of place in order to produce good estimates of population characteristics for small as well as large civil divisions.

Matrix sampling is a more complex content sampling scheme, in which several different long forms are used, each sent to a subsample of the census universe. Each form includes a different subset of the full set of content items. The subsets are designed in such a way that there is adequate sample size for each item and so that combinations of items for which cross-tabulations are important appear together on some subset of the forms. The use of matrix sampling in the decennial census is not new: it was used in both the 1950 and 1960 censuses for the housing sample items (see Bureau of the Census, 1965; Goldfield, 1992).

Matrix sampling was also used extensively in the 1970 census for both population and housing items. There were two long forms; one was sent to 5 percent of households, and the other was sent to 15 percent of households. Some questions appeared on both forms and, thus, were asked of 20 percent of households. Matrix sampling was quite important in 1970 because this was the first census from which data tapes were provided to users to do their own analysis. (In 1950 and 1960, only printed reports prepared by the Census Bureau were generally available.) Users found matrix sampling in 1970 to be a nuisance because of the limitations on cross-tabulations and the need to access multiple data products (e.g., there were two PUMS [(public-use microdata sample)] files, one for each long form).

Matrix sampling for content, the "multiple sample forms" census design element, is attractive because it can reduce respondent burden while yielding high overall content. Content here refers to statistical information on various joint, conditional, and marginal distributions of census items (Bureau of the Census, 1993c, especially p. 20; Griffin and Cresce, 1993; Miskura, 1993a).

 The specific advantages of matrix sampling for long-form items are that respondent burden can be more evenly distributed; each item may be included only as often as necessary (it is not necessary to have the same sampling rate for every item), and there is an opportunity to expand content by asking more questions without making any single form excessively long. Matrix sampling also has some liabilities that will have to be addressed in order to determine whether its use in the census will be beneficial: sample size for some cross-tabulations may be decreased; the best estimates for tabulations and cross-tabulations for some items will require use of statistical estimation methods; analysis of the resulting data products will be more complicated than with a single sample; and costs may increase due to increased content and operational complexity. The latter two problems were also noted by

Citro and Cohen (1985:261).

Current plans appear to provide for tests of a method that would have four or five sample forms, each with a lesser level of respondent burden than the previous long form. Specific content--items to be sampled--will be determined at a later date. Current plans also call for simulation tests based on the 1990 census long-form data. Marginal tabulations for each item are available on the basis of every response containing that item. Similarly, cross-tabulations for pairs or larger combinations of items may be based on forms on which those items appear together. More efficient estimates of tabulations and cross-tabulations require statistical estimation to combine marginal and cross-tabulated information from different samples. Optimal design for the proposed implementation must take into account the correlations among items to be collected on a sample basis. Items that are independent can be placed on separate forms. Items that are almost perfectly correlated require little overlapping or splicing across forms. But for the many items that are neither independent nor perfectly correlated in the total population or major population subgroups, these design issues warrant investigation.

Matrix sampling may prove valuable as a method for obtaining additional information for a given level of cost and respondent burden, although the ability to cross-classify this information would be somewhat diminished. Many of the questions that must be answered in order to plan and evaluate a matrix sampling scheme can best be attacked through simulations based on 1990 data, because those data provide a reasonable approximation to the universe of items from which matrix sampling will draw.

Both item content and pertinent levels of geography for this content must be examined simultaneously in simulation experiments. In addition to statistical design for item selection and overlapping or splicing (by pertinent geographical units), sampling protocols that stratify by levels of geography (e.g., by state) must be considered. Sample stratification must also be considered in relation to subnational needs for census content.

The optimal design of multiple forms has to be investigated carefully, using the 1990 census long-form data to simulate likely outcomes for the 2000 census. Such simulations need to take account of interactions among items used (not just pairwise correlation or association). Because almost all census content items (occupation, labor force status, etc.) are most useful for levels of geography, such as states, counties, cities, and minor civil divisions, the correlation structure and conditional interactions must be examined within pertinent levels of geography. The relevant variance comparisons can also be simulated reasonably well with analyses based on the 1990 census long-form data. The 1995 census test cannot provide decisive information on variances of interest because the correlation structure within and across pertinent geographic areas cannot be simulated from a test census conducted at only four sites.

Research must also be carried out to examine the operational feasibility, cost, and effects on bias and variance of the implementation of matrix sampling in combination with other basic census designs under consideration. For example, if nonresponse follow-up is conducted partly on a sample basis, it is not obvious how to select sample forms for the target samples to be used in sample nonresponse follow-up. In fact, these interactions may be problematical even if only a single sample form is used. While simulations with 1990 data may partly answer questions of this sort, testing in 1995 will be necessary to fully explore these issues, especially those related to operations and costs.

> **Recommendation 2.7:** The Census Bureau should continue research on possible matrix sampling designs, using the 1990 census data to simulate tabulations and crosstabulations. Design(s) that appear most promising should be tested in 1995 to permit evaluation of their performance in combination with other census design features under test.

Finally, matrix sampling is only one of the methods under consideration that are designed to increase or retain census content. The other main method is continuous data collection through samples on monthly or annual bases throughout the decade, perhaps using matrix sampling. Research on variance and bias, imputation for nonresponse, and other statistical issues should be carried out to make comparisons between matrix sampling and continuous measurement. However, we are not sure that it is possible to simulate such factors with 1990 census data. (Proposals for continuous data collection are discussed more fully in Chapter 5.)

STATISTICAL ESTIMATION

Census design features being considered for 2000 will create new demands for statistical estimation methods. Each of the methods described previously in this chapter--sampling or truncation of nonresponse follow-up, coverage estimation, and matrix sampling--requires a corresponding estimation strategy and research on particular aspects of implementation.

Nonresponse follow-up sampling. Estimates must be obtained of numbers and characteristics of persons and households who would have been found in each block during nonresponse follow-up had all households been included in the nonresponse follow-up sample. The information that can be used in this estimation process includes the number and characteristics of persons found in nonresponse follow-up in sample blocks or households, the number of unresolved nonresponse addresses in the nonsample blocks or households, and the number and characteristics of persons found during unsampled census operations (mailback and other presampling responses).

Truncation. Truncation increases the number of persons who are not directly enumerated and therefore must be statistically estimated or assigned. As this number becomes larger, the demands on estimation for accuracy become more stringent.

Coverage estimation. Methods such as models or poststratification schemes must be developed for describing patterns of undercoverage. Sample sizes will probably be such that direct estimates are possible only for fairly large aggregates. Estimation of population and characteristics for smaller aggregates will require development of such indirect estimation methods as synthetic estimation and empirical Bayes smoothing. At the most detailed level, methods will be required for incorporating estimated persons and households into individual blocks, creating units with realistic characteristics in such a way that additivity is maintained across levels of geography.

Additional information sources. Inclusion of new information sources into the census, such as administrative records and multiple response modes, may create new demands on estimation methodologies.

Matrix sampling. As noted above, the use of matrix sampling implies the use of estimation to combine information from various sample forms efficiently and to estimate cross-tabulations for which there is little or no information in the sample data.

Necessary research on statistical estimation divides roughly into three phases. In the first phase, which is now underway and continues until the major design decisions have been made for the 1995 census test, estimation research focuses on broadening the range of possibilities for the use of sampling and other statistically based techniques. In this phase, preliminary assessments can be obtained of the expected precision for various designs. In the second phase, roughly coinciding with the planning, execution, and processing of the 1995 census test, the emphasis shifts to developing methods needed for the selected designs and methodological features. In the final phase, beginning with assessment of the 1995 census test and continuing through the decade, the selected estimation methods will have to be consolidated, optimized, validated, and made both theoretically and operationally robust. This last process will ensure that they can stand up to critical scrutiny and to problems that may arise in the course of the 2000 census. In this phase, work will also continue on selecting estimation procedures required for the production of all census products.

Recommendation 2.8: The Census Bureau should vigorously pursue research on statistical estimation now and throughout the decade. Topics should include nonresponse follow-up sampling, coverage estimation, incorporation of varied information sources (including administrative records), indirect estimation for small areas, and matrix sampling.

Official statistics have progressed over the century from a narrow focus on simple tabulations of population characteristics to provision of a range of census products, including complex tabulations and sample microdata files. Analytical uses of these data require availability of both point estimates and measures of uncertainty. When complex statistical methods, such as complex sampling schemes, indirect estimation, and imputation are used in creating census products, users will not be able to derive valid measures of uncertainty by elementary methods, and they may not have adequate information in the published or available products to derive these measures. It therefore becomes the responsibility of the data producers to facilitate estimation of uncertainty.

"Total error models" have been used by the Census Bureau to measure uncertainty in the outcomes of the census and the contributions of the various sources of error to this uncertainty (Hansen et al., 1961). More recently, a total error model was developed for estimation of uncertainty in adjusted estimates based on the 1990 census and PES (Mulry and Spencer, 1993). Such models take into account both sampling errors in the estimates and potential biases stemming from the regular census and from coverage estimation. Bias can arise, for example, from use of several response modes or from differences among response times. Similar models may be a useful tool for evaluating uncertainty in integrated estimates from a complex census in the year 2000.

Recommendation 2.9: The Census Bureau should develop methods for measuring and modeling all sources of error in the census and for showing uncertainty in published tabulations or otherwise enabling users to estimate uncertainty.

3

RESPONSE AND COVERAGE

Much of the Census Bureau's research on response and coverage for the year 2000 census addresses two main criticisms raised about the 1990 census: the high unit cost of the census and the increase in the differential undercount by race. One of the most important findings of the 1990 census--the increasing diversity of the United States--also identifies one reason for its difficulties. While many people continue to be persuaded by appeals based on citizenship and a common national duty, and many have the skills and motivation to respond to the census mail questionnaire, a sizable and perhaps increasing proportion appear to be motivated primarily by local interests and appeals, demand control over portions of the census process or outcomes, or require specialized help or media in order to participate. If the trends uncovered by the 1990 census continue, as expected, the 2000 census will face even greater obstacles. A recognition that the United States is simply and fundamentally becoming ever more difficult to count must be incorporated into planning for 2000 in order to develop viable strategies and the organizational and political consensus to implement them.

Controlling costs and reducing the differential undercount in 2000 may require a massive reorientation--both conceptually and organizationally. The 1990 census attempted to universally apply a standard, and standardized, approach, but the outcome was a differential undercount. Furthermore, standardization necessarily broke down in many areas, particularly those in which response to the mail questionnaire was low, as enumerators with only brief training were sent out and ultimately empowered to make last-ditch enumerations, using procedures known as last resort and closeout that permitted contacting persons who were not residents of the household. The 1990 experience with coverage improvement programs--such as the housing coverage check and the second phase of the parolee-probationer check--suggests that the real alternative to planning different approaches for different populations may be using different approaches in a haphazard manner. Instead, we believe that a system could be designed that is flexible enough to help reduce the differential undercount yet maintain important aspects of standardization (such as definitions of household membership).

Some components of the research on the topics discussed in this chapter seem designed mainly to control costs by increasing response to the initial mail questionnaire and are fairly traditional. But other portions of the research program, particularly those aimed at "targeting barriers to enumeration," have the potential to help produce more innovative approaches and possibly reduce the differential undercount.

The most developed component of the Census Bureau's research on response issues addresses the problem of reducing the unit cost of each response by increasing the number of people who return the mail questionnaire. Although increasing the initial response rate may leave the differential undercount unchanged--or even exacerbate it somewhat--a higher initial response rate means better quality data, fewer nonrespondents to follow up, and better control over cost. For these reasons, the experiments demonstrating that better design of the questionnaires and sending advance letters, reminder cards, and replacement questionnaires can improve response rates in a census have had an important role to play. And these experiments have also given the Census Bureau needed experience with new operational procedures based on implementation techniques that survey researchers have developed over the last 20 years.

The research program focused on the differential undercount draws on the work of the Census Bureau's Barriers to Enumeration Working Group and has become better developed since the late fall of 1992. What we refer to here as a "program" is really a diverse set of relevant topics and projects that have been collected as the Special Methods Research and Development Program; these projects have been compared to each other and ranked by census data users during a series of Census Bureau consultations with the Commerce Department task force and other census advisory committees. The range of the projects under consideration is important, because some projects address the components of the undercount due to missing households and other projects address components due to missing people within households. In many cases, however, what has been formulated is more a topic than a research project; what is needed is development with the goal of evaluation--experimental evaluation where possible--and cost estimation.

Our review of the research projects addressing response and related coverage issues suggests that the response rate improvement research program has yielded strategies that promise to help control costs in 2000, but that research should now focus on techniques that have potential to reduce the differential undercount. We do not recommend abandoning research on improving initial mail response altogether, given its critical role in controlling costs and in the overall success of the census. But efforts to improve initial mail response should now focus on planning for key instrument and implementation experiments in the 1995 census test. The plans should draw on both research already conducted at the Census Bureau and other findings reported in the literature--for example, on the use of telephone for follow-up--to test the "best" feasible implementation methods. It is not necessary to have a large-scale experiment for every innovation in design or mail-out procedure before the 1995 test.

The remainder of this chapter discusses and makes specific recommendations on a range of topics related to response and coverage issues. We review the extensive response rate improvement research program conducted by the Census Bureau. We also focus attention on proposed research, and four major themes emerge from our discussion.

(1) *Focus on reducing the differential undercount.* We recommend planning and limited experimentation now so that the most promising methods for reducing the differential undercount can, where feasible, be given operational trials and experimental and cost evaluation in the 1995 census test. Narrowing the research program to methods that may reduce the differential undercount is important given the limitations of resources and time, and it can be justified by the more advanced state of research on improving mail response rates. If operational variables associated with response, such as time of receipt and medium used, have been tracked, then much can be learned from analyses of data from the 1980 and 1990 censuses. We urge the Census Bureau to devote resources to activities of this type whenever potentially valuable information can be obtained through alternatives to expensive, large-scale experimentation.

(2) *Go local.* The targeting model and tool kit proposed in the Census Bureau's research program provide for localized, decentralized outreach and enumeration activities. But more may be needed. Because undercounted groups are clustered and because their reasons for not participating may vary greatly by locality, reducing the differential undercount will probably require a major reorientation in the Census Bureau's practice. Outreach and enumeration activities may need to be more decentralized than current field offices, which, even when they know where to find undercounted groups, may not have the credibility needed to motivate them to participate. Learning how to localize outreach, promotion, and enumeration should be central to planning for the 1995 census test, as should the development of designs to evaluate the success and to estimate costs of such efforts. Good procedures for eliminating duplicate records (see Chapter 1) are also needed if the Census Bureau is to be able to manage more flexible enumeration procedures that respond to local needs (e.g., filling out a form in the shopping mall) without losing accuracy.

(3) *Develop a plan for national and locally based outreach and promotion.* Messages are needed that will motivate members of groups that are hard to enumerate. Promotional efforts should include gaining access to local media markets. Such strategies may both enhance the response to the initial mailout among undercounted populations and support more targeted enumeration efforts.

(4) *Develop and test the application of residence rules for both mail and telephone implementation.* Coverage errors within households are response errors. Clearer definitions and less ambiguous questions are needed to help respondents provide more accurate answers. Because the 2000 census is likely to include more use of telephone--either as a primary response mode or to follow up nonrespondents--it is also important that a telephone version of these new questions be developed and mode differences examined.

RESPONSE IMPROVEMENT RESEARCH

Taken as a whole, the Census Bureau's response improvement program attempts a coordinated approach to a wide range of issues, and the program clearly has the potential to mitigate the decline in mail return rates or even to increase the rates. The use of a "respondent friendly" questionnaire, an advance notification letter, a reminder postcard, and a replacement questionnaire are all methods that have been widely adopted in surveys, and their extension to the census is overdue and promising.

Response Rate Improvement

The Census Bureau conducted the Simplified Questionnaire Test (SQT) in April 1992. Its primary purpose was to compare the final mail completion rates for four alternative short-form questionnaire designs (booklet, micro, micro with Social Security number, and roster) to the 1990 census short-form questionnaire in a survey environment (Bryant, 1992). The test yielded an increase of 3.4 percentage points in response rate using the respondent-friendly version of the 1990 short form.

The Implementation Test (IT) was designed to test the benefits of three components in the mail implementation plan for the short-form sample--a prenotice letter, a stamped return envelope, and a reminder postcard (Bureau of the Census, 1992d). The IT was carried out by the Census Bureau in October 1992 and found that use of a prenotice letter and reminder card together produced a gain of 12.7 percentage points in the response rate. On the basis of the SQT and IT results, Census Bureau statisticians estimate that the use of a replacement questionnaire will increase response by approximately 10 percentage points. Although it is less clear whether any of the techniques investigated in this program will reduce the differential undercount, any increase in routine mail responses improves data quality and helps to control costs.

Because these treatments were not all tested in combination with one another, we cannot confidently assess the degree to which they are additive. Also, the magnitude of these treatment effects in the environment of an actual census year is unknown. Nevertheless, the strength of the experimental findings suggests that these features are likely to have a significant positive effect on response rates in the next decennial census.

Mail and Telephone Mode Test (MTMT). The MTMT was designed to examine whether offering respondents the option of calling in a response or receiving a replacement questionnaire increases the response rate. The treatments vary in when the offer is made, and one treatment (the "preference" treatment) allows respondents to call when they first receive the form. The experiment was conducted in April 1992, and initial results suggest that offering people the opportunity to call in for telephone enumeration does not increase the total response rate. If the complete MTMT results bear out this preliminary finding, offering people more "high-tech" response modes--such as the fax--that require them to take the initiative in responding are similarly unlikely to increase the total response rate.

We have two concerns about the MTMT. One is that it may discourage research into ways that the telephone is more likely to be used successfully. As it has in sample surveys, the telephone will probably prove itself a useful follow-up tool in the 2000 census--for reminding people to return their questionnaires and for completing cases without sending an enumerator to the field.

A second concern about experiments using the telephone is that because residence rules are complex, answers to the self-administered mail questionnaire (which displays the residence rules) may differ from answers to the version of the questionnaire used in computer-assisted telephone interviewing (CATI) (in which the rules may or may not be read to the respondent). Furthermore, the mode effect may vary depending on whether a respondent interviewed by CATI is looking at the questionnaire or not. During the MTMT, people were encouraged to have the census form in front of them when they call to be interviewed, but this result, obviously, cannot be guaranteed. In the MTMT a self-selected group was enumerated by telephone; therefore, the MTMT cannot be used to estimate the possible mode effects. And estimating the effects of mode on within-household coverage is essential if people are to be allowed to respond to the census using different modes. In addition, procedures to eliminate duplicate cases are critical to maintaining accuracy when households are allowed to respond by modes other than mail.

Appeals and Long Form Experiment (ALFE). This experiment was conducted in July 1993. The first component of this experiment tests the effects of two different motivational appeals, one emphasizing the mandatory nature of the census, the other stressing the benefits of census participation. The second component tests several respondent-friendly versions of the 1990 long form. The key substantive issue explored by this experiment is how to better motivate participation. This is a question that also affects other components of the census (see discussion below of outreach and promotion). Although we agree that research on how to motivate participation is important, we believe that it should be integrated with research on how to motivate participation by members of undercounted groups. In addition, the 1995 census test should build on the results of ALFE and further test the use ofmotivational appeals.

At a more specific level, the description of ALFE notes that using a statement that response is mandatory may irritate or threaten some respondents. If this research is pursued further (for example, in the 1995 census test), we suggest a treatment in which the statement that participation is mandatory is added during follow-up (e.g., with the reminder card) and not included in the initial mailing.

Multiple Response Modes. The original goal of "expanding response modes" now appears to be limited to telephone, which is the most "high-tech" mode listed on page 1 of the "Summary of Research Projects" (Bureau of the Census, 1993f). Some of the results from the MTMT, particularly the use of the telephone in the "preference" treatment, in which the initial mailing invites response by telephone, can be plausibly generalized to more specialized modes, such as fax. Although we see important possibilities for using the telephone, particularly in following up those who do not respond by mail (see below), accepting telephone responses requires research on methods to eliminate duplication of records. Research to eliminate duplicate records is probably also essential for some components of the tool kit (described in the next section). In addition, as noted above, accepting telephone responses when the respondent does not have the census form available requires development of a telephone instrument.

A complicating feature of these experiments is that crucial features of the 2000 census--such as what information is needed to eliminate duplicate records, the method for capturing data, and the final operational form of residence rules--must necessarily remain in doubt, even while research about improving the mail response rate proceeds. We are concerned, therefore, that some of these features may interact with the experimental manipulations. Such interactions could compromise projections of response rates for the 2000 census. The feature of most concern in this respect is the operational form of the residence rules, which can affect the entire design of the questionnaire (see discussion below).

> **Recommendation 3.1:** At this time, the Census Bureau should not initiate any further large-scale experiments designed to improve the initial mail response rate. Instead, response improvement research should now consolidate findings from research conducted to date in order to design experiments for the 1995 census test. The primary objective of these experiments should be to identify optimal field procedures that combine features such as advance notification, replacement questionnaires, and telephone follow-up.

Telephone Follow-Up

Although the response improvement research has focused on the initial mail response, planning and operational tests for 1995 should also include an evaluation of telephone follow-up to improve mail response. Telephone follow-up is likely to be more productive than the use of the telephone tested in MTMT; outgoing telephone calls can be used both to remind people to return their forms and to complete the enumeration by telephone (for example, one week after a reminder call) using a CATI system. Current plans call for the telephone number of the household to be added to the master address file (MAF) for the 2000 census (Bureau of the Census, 1992e). This suggests that some of the planning needed to include telephone follow-up in the 1995 census test is already under way. The idea of conducting telephone follow-up has surfaced periodically and was even tested successfully in the 1980 census (Ferrari and Bailey, 1983). Preliminary results indicated that the use of telephone provided several advantages over follow-up by enumerators: lower costs per completed interview, lower item nonresponse rates for many items, and fewer duplicate questionnaires. Using telephone follow-up when possible would also reduce the number of enumerators required and make it possible to improve their quality by being more selective and by providing more extensive training. Furthermore, enumerators at telephone facilities would be centrally managed, scheduled, and monitored.

    One disadvantage of telephone follow-up in 1980 was that directory listings were missing or outdated (Ferrari and Bailey, 1983). But telephone numbers could be added to the MAF using commercial firms that match telephone numbers with addresses, and this may improve the quality of telephone numbers. The 1995 census test can also build on other results from the 1980 experiment--for example, the finding that more questionnaires than expected were returned after cases were selected for telephone follow-up.

> **Recommendation 3.2:** The prospect of having telephone numbers for a large percentage of households in the 2000 census is a potentially important development that should be explored in the Census Bureau's 1995 test--for example, by using the telephone for reminder calls and nonresponse follow-up.

    In addition to using telephones for reminder calls and other nonresponse follow-up, the role of the telephone in designs such as SuperCensus or CensusPlus must also be examined. And if the telephone is to be used more frequently, the possibility of mode effects on enumeration (that is, on coverage) must be assessed (see discussion below). This is particularly important because telephone enumeration will be more likely among some groups than others. The differential biases associated with different modes can be accounted for in the models used to estimate the population unless mode effects can be estimated and controlled.

TARGETING MODEL AND TOOL KIT

    The heart of the projects proposed by the Census Bureau's Special Methods Working Group is the development of the targeting model and tool kit. The targeting model is conceived as a predictive model that would identify geographic areas where enumeration barriers are likely to be present in 2000 and where deployment of special enumeration methods might be particularly useful. The model would also identify the types of enumeration problems that are anticipated, so that suitable methods would be drawn from the tool kit.

    "Tool kit" refers to the collection of special methods--for example, team enumeration, "blitz" tactics, and bilingual enumerators--available for deployment in hard-to-enumerate areas. Use of the tool kit could also involve specialized outreach procedures and decisions at the headquarters level on mailout-mailback procedures, allocation of staff and resources, and differential pay rates and incentives for census workers.

    Both the targeting model and the tool kit represent large development efforts, and the tool kit encompasses many potential research and evaluation projects. Presumably, the model and tool kit will be developed together, because one need only target barriers for which one has a potential solution in the tool kit. The development of the tool kit itself requires that the Census Bureau develop systematic distinctions between promotion and outreach activities--between building awareness and developing motivation--and also identify which promotion and outreach activities should be conducted at the local and national levels.

Development of the targeting model should use the findings of the ethnographic research reports (e.g., de la Puente, 1993) that identify many structural conditions that make coverage of households and of people within households more difficult. For example, geographic areas with high-cost housing and low-income residents probably create conditions in which unrelated people crowd into small or irregular dwellings, and enumeration difficulties result. The Census Bureau is currently engaged in research that attempts to identify which demographic and housing characteristics--such as racial composition, size of household, and tenure-- might be valuable in predicting which areas are particularly at risk for low mail response rates, high undercount rates, or high coverage error rates.

The targeting model and tool kit will require flexible implementation because the targeting model will not be based on current data, and the tool kit should be responsive to actual field conditions. The efforts and resources required to develop the targeting model, however, appear to be so massive that there is some risk that the tool kit, and the coordination between the targeting model and the tool kit may be underdeveloped and underevaluated. The basis for our concern is the same as that for our recommendation that the Census Bureau plan to "go local" in outreach, promotion, and (to some extent) enumeration by developing locally targeted outreach and promotion efforts: reducing the differential undercount requires decentralization and flexibility. Evaluation of the targeting model should consider who within the field management structure is given access to the model and its results and what tool kit resources are made available to field staff. (Our concerns about these issues are discussed more fully in the next sections.)

The targeting model and tool kit constitute a strategy for taking the census, and further research and development must proceed from this perspective. Currently, the targeting model and tool kit are presented more as field management tools rather than as full components of a census design. But the tool kit will ultimately include a set of enumeration, communication, outreach, and data collection methods, each of which requires development and experimental evaluation. We suggest that the various constituent components of the targeting model and the tool kit be specified more completely to help staff in identifying the kind of development and evaluation that each requires.

We believe it is particularly important that plans to evaluate the effectiveness of the targeting model and of components of the tool kit should be incorporated into the 1995 census test. Ideally, the 1995 census test would incorporate a trial of the targeting model and an evaluation--for example, by examining response rates by area. Even if the targeting model is not fully developed by 1995, techniques that are planned for the tool kit can be evaluated experimentally before, during, and after the census test. Posttest evaluation surveys can be used to determine whether people were aware of outreach and promotion efforts and can help in evaluating the effectiveness of such efforts. Components of the tool kit should be tested in experiments such as those used to test ways of improving mail response rates. It may be possible to incorporate some tests into other field projects (e.g., experiments examining ways to improve coverage). It seems likely that the development and testing of the targeting model and tool kit will continue after the 1995 census test, and even after the 2000 census, and planning should take this schedule into account.

OUTREACH AND PROMOTION

The outreach and promotion program for the 1990 census was the most intensive to date for a decennial census. For the first time, a multifaceted mass media campaign addressed several traditionally undercounted groups as well as the general public. The community-based Census Awareness and Products Program (CAPP) was enhanced and began operations farther in advance of census day than in 1980. Programs were conducted that worked through national civic and religious organizations, schools, Head Start agencies, governmental units, and business organizations.

Based on an analysis of the data collected in the 1990 Outreach and Evaluation Survey, Bates and Whitford (1991) concluded that the Census Bureau's 1990 outreach and promotion program achieved many of its goals. The Advertising Council's mass media campaign received wide exposure, and it achieved the third highest media presence around census day in the six media markets where the coverage was monitored. By census day, over 90 percent of the population had recently heard or read something about the census, although the campaign was less effective in reaching blacks than whites and Hispanics.

Outreach and publicity may also help the census mail response rate; data from the Outreach and Evaluation Survey indicate that in 1990 the mail return rates of respondents with high awareness of census operations and knowledge of census uses were 15 to 20 percentage points higher than respondents with low awareness and knowledge (Bates and Whitford, 1991). (We cite these results with the standard caution that the question of whether these associations reflect causal relationships cannot be answered without considering potential interaction effects and controlling for other variables in a designed experiment.) Nevertheless, the mail response rate in 1990 was 10 percentage points below the 1980 census, and the differential undercount between blacks and nonblacks was the highest since the Census Bureau began estimating coverage in 1940 (U.S. General Accounting Office, 1992). Although there are undoubtedly many social factors that contributed to the response rate decline, it is also possible that the Census Bureau's 1990 outreach and promotion campaign did a better job of *announcing* the census than it did of *persuading* people to participate. Regardless, it seems clear that an even more intensive--and effective--outreach and promotion program will need to be designed, tested, and successfully implemented in the 2000 census if the Census Bureau is to prevent further erosion of census participation rates that began declining in 1970.

Components of Decennial Census Outreach and Promotion

The various components of the Census Bureau's decennial census outreach and promotion program include the establishment of a temporary Census Promotion Office and the conduct of a media campaign, national and local outreach efforts, and research and evaluation projects. In the last two censuses, Census Promotion Office has opened 2 years prior to the decennial census and closed after census operations were completed. It appears that the primary function of this office is to coordinate the media campaign with the Advertising Council and to oversee various national outreach programs conducted to promote the upcoming census. (The Census Bureau has a permanent Public Information Office, but it is not directly involved in decennial census promotion.)

In every census since 1950, the Census Bureau has relied on the Advertising Council to design and conduct the media campaign. (Working through advertising agencies that volunteer their time, the Advertising Council regularly conducts mass media advertising campaigns on a pro bono basis for government and nonprofit agencies.) In 1990 the Advertising Council for the first time designed multiple campaigns to target selected minorities (blacks, Hispanics, and Asian/Pacific Islanders) as well as the general public.

The principal national outreach program to undercounted groups is the National Services Program (NSP). Conducted by the Data User Services Division, the NSP is a continuing outreach and data dissemination program aimed at national organizations that represent undercounted minorities. The goal of the NSP is to secure the support of the national organizations and their local and regional chapters in efforts to encourage participation by the minority communities they represent. The Census Bureau also conducts a variety of national outreach activities close to census day: these include programs that target a variety of organizations, schools, governmental units and agencies, and private-sector corporations. The principal program for local outreach is the Census Awareness and Products Program (CAPP). Administered by the Census Bureau's Field Division, this program is activated a year or two prior to census day and deactivated shortly afterwards. In 1990 there were about 280 CAPP staff across the country, working out of the regional field offices.

The Census Bureau's decennial census outreach and promotion program does not include a structured plan for conducting research and development work. The absence of a permanent office responsible for decennial census outreach and promotion militates against sustaining an ongoing research program during the decade between censuses. Also, the Advertising Council does not permit its clients to undertake or commission media research on their own. The Census Bureau does, however, undertake retrospective research to evaluate decennial census outreach and promotion. Examples from the 1990 census include the Outreach Evaluation Survey, the Telephone Survey of Census Participation, the Survey of 1990 Census Participation, and the National Service Program Structured Debriefings.

The Special Methods Working Group of the Year 2000 Research and Development staff has expressed interest in outreach research for the 2000 census, but this type of research does not appear to have a very high priority within the Census Bureau. We note, for example, that only 3 projects related to outreach and promotion are included in the list of 17 proposed special methods projects (Bureau of the Census, 1993g). One project is a study of methods to enumerate American Indians and Alaska native populations, which may include an outreach and promotion program. Another is a comparative study of paid versus pro bono advertising, and the third is a cost-benefit analysis to determine if the Census Bureau should retain an outside public relations firm. The Commerce Department Task Force committees and other advisory groups have assigned these projects priority rankings of 7, 15, and 16 respectively (out of 17), and we understand that it is doubtful whether the 2000 census research budget can support them.

We are concerned that the responsibility for outreach and promotion is split among several different units within the Census Bureau. We believe that the effectiveness and efficiency of the Census Bureau's decennial census outreach and promotion program could be improved if a permanent office were established and staffed with advertising and public relations professionals. This office would be responsible for planning, researching, and developing all outreach and promotion activities and for overseeing the implementation of the decennial program. It should be a permanent office to provide continuity between censuses and to monitor an ongoing national and local outreach and promotion program during the decade. The office should also be nonpartisan and insulated from political influence. Because the Census Bureau already has a permanent Public Information Office, we suggest that the Census Bureau consider expanding the mission of this office to include responsibility for the decennial census outreach and promotion program.

Although the establishment of a permanent decennial census outreach and promotion office would centralize the overall responsibility for outreach and promotion activities, it does not follow that such activities would become more focused on the national rather than the local level. Nor should they, as we argue below; a principal objective of the new central office should be to enhance outreach efforts at the local level. Just as the centralized Field Division is responsible for all data collection operations conducted by the regional offices, so a centralized decennial census outreach and promotion office would design, monitor, and support all field outreach activities conducted through those regional offices.

The one outreach and promotion activity that should not be consolidated under the purview of the new office is evaluation research. To preserve independence, this type of research should continue to be undertaken by other units within the Census Bureau, such as the Center for Survey Methods Research.

Recommendation 3.3: The Census Bureau should assign overall responsibility for decennial census outreach and promotion to a centralized, permanent, and nonpartisan office. The Census Bureau should consider expanding the mission of the extant Public Information Office to include this charge. Evaluation of outreach and promotion programs should be conducted by an independent unit within the Census Bureau.

Customized Local Outreach Programs and CAPP

One of the principal objectives of the 2000 census is to reduce the differential undercount by improving the participation rate of blacks, Hispanics, American Indians, Alaska natives, and other traditionally undercounted groups. It follows, then, that a key goal for the 2000 census outreach and promotion program is to identify ways of reaching the undercounted groups with a campaign that will not just announce the census, but also motivate them to participate.

It seems clear that the only way to reach the undercounted minorities effectively is to develop customized programs that use local channels for outreach and promotion. This message was repeated over and over again by the speakers at the recent Research Conference on Undercounted Ethnic Populations sponsored by the Census Bureau. It is also found in the Census Bureau's own research on the effectiveness of outreach efforts with ethnic minorities (see, e.g., Newhouse, 1992) and in our analysis of the Census Bureau's 1990 ethnographic research (see section below, "Hard-to-Enumerate Populations"). The local programs should be developed in close consultation with the minority groups to which they are directed. The programs should also be designed to maximize the participation of minority organizations and representative in their implementation.

As many of the ethnic group representatives at the Research Conference on Undercounted Ethnic Populations pointed out, it is important to maintain some level of outreach with the undercounted ethnic minorities on an ongoing basis, in order to establish the trust necessary to ensure their participation at census time. Outreach and promotion on an ongoing basis would include not only efforts in the latter part of the decade to support decennial counting, but also postcensal feedback on census results and assistance with using census data. The CAPP program appears to be a good vehicle through which to establish and maintain relationships with the undercounted minorities at the local level. Therefore, we encourage the Census Bureau to expand this program further and support it on a continuing basis.

Overall responsibility for this program should be vested in a central office responsible for all decennial census outreach and promotion (see Recommendation 3.3 above); however, the program should continue to be implemented through the regional field offices. The CAPP staff assigned to the regional offices would be responsible for implementing customized local outreach programs. Statistics Canada coordinates all outreach programs through a central office that maintains links to provinces and local communities through regional offices. The Census Bureau might consider a similar approach.

We do not think that an ongoing CAPP program need be prohibitively expensive. On the contrary, most minority groups have a vested interest in ensuring that all of their constituents are counted at census time, and, as pointed out by several presenters at the Research Conference on Undercounted Ethnic Populations, local volunteer help is often available from the undercounted minorities themselves. Staffing may not need to be uniform over time. One or two core CAPP staff per regional office might be supplemented with temporary help during the period around the decennial year. Given the potential of customized local outreach programs to reduce the differential undercount, we believe that the relatively modest cost of expanding the CAPP program would prove to be a wise investment.

Recommendation 3.4: The Census Bureau should commit the resources necessary to develop and implement customized, local outreach programs to target the traditionally undercounted ethnic minorities. The Census Awareness and Products Program (CAPP) should be expanded and sustained on an ongoing basis, so that it can serve as the primary vehicle for the design and implementation of these outreach programs.

Research and Development Program and the 1995 Census Test

Outreach and promotion research is not a principal component of the Census Bureau's 2000 census research and development program. We believe that the low priority assigned to this aspect of decennial operations is unfortunate in view of its importance to the success of the next census.

In our opinion, the Census Bureau should establish an ongoing research and development program for outreach and promotion. The program should be designed and conducted by a new decennial census outreach and promotion office. Two areas that should be explored are media advertising and local outreach. The advertising research program would focus on such issues as developing effective advertising messages and strategies for the undercounted minority groups, making increased use of local and regional campaigns, and using paid advertising to supplement the public service announcement campaign. The local outreach component of the research and development program would focus on developing and evaluating the customized local outreach programs described above.

The 1995 census test offers an excellent opportunity to evaluate alternative outreach and promotion strategies. If possible, the Census Bureau should include in the 1995 census test some experimental designs to evaluate alternative media campaigns and local outreach programs. At a minimum, the Census Bureau should implement the most promising of the campaigns and programs and then conduct an evaluation of their effectiveness. One way to do this would be to conduct an Outreach Evaluation Survey in 1995 patterned after the one conducted in connection with the 1990 census.

Recommendation 3.5: The Census Bureau should establish an ongoing research and development program for decennial census outreach and promotion. The 1995 census test provides an excellent opportunity to conduct and evaluate promising media campaigns and local outreach programs.

National Media Campaign

An important issue confronting the Census Bureau is whether to continue to rely on the Advertising Council to design and implement the national media campaign. As noted above, the Advertising Council's rules prohibit clients from commissioning any media research on their own. The Council also does not permit clients to supplement the pro bono campaign with any paid advertising. Thus, the Census Bureau is entirely dependent on the Advertising Council's pro bono campaign for its media research and advertising.

Because the Advertising Council depends on volunteer labor, we are concerned that its pro bono campaign may not include the same level of media research that large commercial advertisers have found beneficial. For example, the leading advertising agencies evaluate commercials by using sophisticated technology that continuously measures a focus group's response to a proposed commercial message. However, this type of research is expensive and may not be included within the scope of a pro bono campaign.

We also understand that there is a growing feeling among certain charitable organizations that national public service announcement campaigns are losing their effectiveness. One theory of this change is that U.S. society has become so diverse and complex that people are increasingly narrowing their focus to the community in which they live. As a consequence, there is a movement among pro bono advertisers away from the national campaigns toward increased use of local campaigns.

Certainly the Census Bureau must continue to rely on public service announcements run on a pro bono basis; it would be prohibitively expensive to launch an equivalent campaign on a strictly fee-for-service basis. However, the Census Bureau could discontinue use of the Advertising Council and instead work directly with local and regional agencies. This approach would allow the Census Bureau to undertake a paid media research program to identify the most effective advertising messages. It would also mean that the national campaign would include a collection of local and regional campaigns that might be more effective in reaching the communities to which they are directed.

Finally, this approach would allow the Census Bureau to supplement pro bono advertising with paid advertising--especially in hard-to-enumerate communities where a pro bono campaign may not provide sufficient or appropriate media exposure (Committee on National Statistics, 1978). We believe that the additional cost involved may be more than offset by the increase in response among the traditionally undercounted groups, with a corresponding reduction in the differential undercount. We note in this regard that Statistics Canada is a strong proponent of paid advertising: it was discontinued in 1986 as a cost-saving measure, but then promptly reinstated after a decline in participation.

Recommendation 3.6: The Census Bureau should evaluate the use of the Advertising Council to conduct the census media campaign. The Census Bureau should consider the alternatives of working directly with local and regional agencies, undertaking paid media research, and supplementing pro bono advertising with paid advertising in hard-to-enumerate localities.

User-Friendly Help

Starr (1992) analyzed why people called the Census Bureau's toll-free 800 number for help with the 1990 census. We commend this type of research; what better way to improve outreach in the next census than to analyze the problems people reported having in the last one. One of Starr's recommendations is that the Census Bureau consider a menu-driven touchtone call routing system that gives callers the opportunity to select options that address their concerns. We concur that this should be an important area for investigation and research.

Although some users may express frustration with menu-driven systems, these systems have grown rapidly in popularity, presumably because they are efficient and effective ways of serving customer needs. By the year 2000, menu-driven call routing is likely to be standard practice among large, customer-oriented businesses. We encourage the Census Bureau to undertake a literature review, develop a system for use in the 1995 census test or later dress rehearsals, and conduct an evaluation that includes the use of focus groups to assess people's reactions.

> **Recommendation 3.7:** The Census Bureau should investigate developing a menu-driven touchtone call routing system for the 2000 census that gives callers to the Census Bureau's toll-free help line quicker access to the specific assistance they want.

We understand that the Census Bureau's Computer-Assisted Survey Information Collection (CASIC) staff has already begun looking at touchtone technology for various data collection applications. We suggest that the Year 2000 staff contact the CASIC staff for guidance in this area.

HARD-TO-ENUMERATE POPULATIONS

One of the most vexing and costly problems attending the enumeration process is the tendency to undercount minority and immigrant populations. The expense involved in attempting to reduce the differential undercount is considerable. Political pressure to redress the problem is also significant, because the nation's large cities want to ensure that undercounted individuals--often in need of city services--are properly represented in the count. Minority-based community organizations, especially (but not exclusively) those representing Native Americans, are particularly eager to see undercounting of their constituencies minimized because critical support funds from the federal government are often calculated on the basis of census information.

Overall, it is clear that one of the major tasks facing the 2000 census is to minimize the differential undercount through the development of more effective and specialized outreach, promotion, and enumeration methods. The 1995 census test must include some experiments with techniques aimed at the differential undercount in order to make effective cost-benefit analysis possible before the decennial census. One important consideration in assessing costs and benefits is the expense of following up nonrespondents, particularly in areas with low primary response rates. Some special methods, though intensive and costly, may have the potential to reduce the differential undercount and may do so partly by improving primary response rates in historically low response areas, thus reducing the workload and costs associated with nonresponse follow-up operations. Only when such special methods have been properly evaluated will it be possible to tell whether they reduce the differential undercount and help control the costs involved in the follow-up efforts that are implemented when people do not respond to the initial mail questionnaire.

Recognizing the urgency of these problems, the Census Bureau took constructive steps in 1990 to identify the reasons that immigrants and minorities are so hard to enumerate by conducting an alternative enumeration in 29 sample areas of the United States and Puerto Rico. The areas were chosen for their high concentration of particular minority subpopulations, urban and rural, as well as the presence of a large number of undocumented immigrants who are known to fear participating in the census. Experienced ethnographers familiar with the target populations conducted the alternative enumeration. They were able to improve the count by using their existing relationships with members of these communities, familiarity with the native languages of the immigrants, and their knowledge of the special housing practices of the poor--both native and immigrant. Results of these special census projects were compared with the enumerations of the same areas in the 1990 census.

From this comparison the Census Bureau learned a great deal about the sources of undercount and overcount. The summary by Brownrigg and de la Puente (1993) indicates that substantial numbers of erroneous enumerations and omissions occurred at the sites, and the net undercount rates varied considerably. The two extreme cases reported a net undercount of 47 percent and a net overcount of 53 percent; the median net coverage was a small undercount of approximately one percent. Clearly, the sites present very difficult counting conditions (discussed below) that create both types of census error. These errors occasionally cancel out within a geographic area, but they are more likely to result in surpluses of omissions or erroneous enumerations that produce the large variations in net undercount that were observed in 1990. For the affected communities, undercounting is a source of great policy concern with regard to issues of political representation and revenue sharing. The primary task now should be to capitalize on this research and to implement the valuable policy suggestions that emerged from this study in designing the 1995 census test and developing the tool kit of methods for the 2000 census field offices.

Manuel de la Puente's excellent summary of the 29 "ethnographic coverage reports" (de la Puente, 1993) identifies five sources of undercount or overcount: (1) irregular and complex living arrangements; (2) irregular housing; (3) residential mobility; (4) distrust of government; and, (5) limited English proficiency. Almost all of these point to the difference between the underlying norms expressed in the census (nuclear families, discrete households, long-term or permanent residences) and the living arrangements of the nation's minorities, whether foreign born or native. Some of these problems are related to the difficulty of enumerating the population in question: gaining trust, counting all the people in a household, and the like. Others are related to locating dwellings in poverty areas of the nation's cities and rural communities and are of great importance in updating the master address file. The Census Bureau will need to take seriously the policy options proposed by the ethnographic studies for both of these domains.

Irregular and Complex Household Arrangements

The first source of enumeration difficulties involves the irregular and complex household arrangements that typify poor minority and immigrant communities. Households defined as irregular or complex contain unrelated individuals, people who are mobile or present for no other reason than to share the burden of the rent, and multiple nuclear families. Households structured in this fashion become extremely difficult to enumerate accurately. Census rules of residence, which ask the respondent to identify members of their household in relation to "person 1," cannot easily accommodate the composition of these living groups and often contradict the respondent's definitions of family or household. In such cases, residence rules are hard to apply; the individuals who "should" be counted may be absent and thus excluded. As an ethnographer working in rural Marion County, Oregon noted (cited in de la Puente, 1993:4):

> If all members are not present, . . . obtaining the data pertaining to persons outside, asleep, at work, or temporarily absent is virtually impossible. It is as if those persons do not exist.

These households may also contain unrelated males who have assembled solely to cut the cost of the rent, who work long hours, and share living space in very dense fashion--with beds lining the rooms and individuals sleeping in shifts.[1] Nothing, other than expediency and common ethnicity, binds these individuals into anything they would define as a "household" of people related to person 1, with emphasis on the term "related." As Rodriguez and Hagan put the matter (cited in de la Puente

---

[1]In some immigrant communities, this kind of dense subleasing is an important source of income for older immigrants, who build a housing pyramid on the basis of holding a lease and exploiting recent arrivals who have no other options (see Mahler, 1993).

1993:7):

> For recent immigrants from Central America and Mexico, household and family are viewed as the same. Boarders and unrelated individuals are not part of the family and thus not part of the household.

At some sites ethnographers discovered that up to half of the individuals living in complex households of this kind were left out of the census (see, e.g., Romero, 1992). The same pattern of undercount was likely to develop in Haitian households, which were composed of a "core" family and a series of peripheral individuals who are "just passing through," but sometimes stay for years. Chinese families in New York may be equally perplexed by the census definitions of household and may augment those present in a household with relatives who are family (e.g., adult children) but no longer living in the house. Again, the residence rules on the census forms confuse even the willing participant--resulting in undercounts (the Haitian example) and overcounts (the Chinese example).

Irregular and complex household structures are generally to be found wherever there are high housing prices and a concentrated poor population (native or immigrant). This is an important finding in and of itself, for researchers (perhaps including the ethnographers working on this project) are prone to believe that these patterns are expressions of cultural differences. The regularity of the ethnographic findings across ethnic subpopulations and in disparate parts of the U.S. suggest there may be little that is culturally specific about formation of irregular households. Rather, irregular households form in response to structural conditions that bring the poor into areas of expensive housing, resulting in these fairly uniform "irregular" practices. If this is true, then it should be possible for the Census Bureau to identify many of these areas in advance and target special resources for enumeration within them.

Irregular Housing

Irregular housing is the second major source of the undercount, one that presents difficulties in locating housing units, rather than in enumerating the individuals living in them. Brownrigg (1991) estimates that across the 29 sample areas subjected to ethnographic evaluation, perhaps as many as 40 percent of the people who should have been included in the count, but were missed, were missed because the housing unit itself was overlooked or misidentified. Commonly, these dwellings were hidden from public view (in backyards or down rural roads) or were illegally built (and often concealed in single-family homes or garages). Irregular housing also causes overcounts because buildings have multiple addresses, multiple entrances, or are temporary dwellings that move around but have already been counted elsewhere--e.g., trailers in the neighborhood just for the weekend (see de la Puente, 1993:12). Irregular housing goes hand-in-hand with irregular and complex households, thus compounding the enumeration problems discussed above. Families are likely to double up in areas where affordable housing is in short supply, stimulating the construction of illegally converted housing.[2]

The success of the ethnographic teams in locating irregular housing was impressive, particularly when compared with the 1990 census. One case study reported a census undercount of nearly 50 percent, much of which could be attributed to missed housing units. The alternative enumeration was often able to identify these irregular dwellings, drawing upon the detailed knowledge of locally-based ethnographers and/or their skill in cultivating "informants" who could guide them into the nether world of warehouses, back alleys, unscrupulous landlords, crack dens, and other unlikely places for private housing.

Residential Mobility

Residential mobility was the third reason given for enumeration difficulties in the 29 sample areas. Some populations that the census generally undercounts tend to move often, to reside in one place for a shorter period of time than what middle-class citizens think of as the norm, and so to be difficult to enumerate. High residential mobility go hand in hand with seasonal and low-wage labor markets, patterns of return migration, and the pressures of accommodating large numbers of "peripheral" members in a household (who are likely to move when the strain becomes too great). Difficulties with landlords give rise to eviction, resulting in greater mobility for poor people than others. Mahler (1993:8, quoted in de la Puente 1993:22) notes that Salvadoran immigrants move as often as three times a year in search of cheaper housing or jobs or because they are reunited with family members.

These circumstances not only make it difficult to count individuals, it exacerbates the difficulties that many of the native-born and immigrant poor face in applying the residence rules. Are temporary household residents "members"? They may be deemed such if they are also relatives, but otherwise they may be excluded because they are both highly mobile and unrelated. Experimentation with questions that ask about "who stayed here last night" may indicate ways in which these undercount problems can be attacked, since this formulation captures the mobile and the unrelated (an undercount problem) and may also cut down on the overcount of those who are kin but not living in that household on census day.

---

[2]Descriptions of these areas leave little doubt that they can be forbidding places for enumerators to survey. Ethnographers were sometimes exposed to threats to their physical safety.

Distrust of Government

Distrust of, or ambivalence toward, the government is another cause of undercounts. In the 29 communities surveyed, many members of the target populations believe they have little to gain in cooperating with the census and fear the possible consequences of yielding information--particularly if they are among the large number of undocumented immigrants or participants in the underground economy. Contending with this problem proved difficult for the ethnographers who worked on this special project, for they were rarely equipped to survey drug enclaves, shanty towns, and the like. They had to contend with the dangers of the street and, perhaps more important, the reticence of ordinary (law-abiding) individuals living under these conditions to open their doors to strangers.

It is clear that many people in immigrant and native-born minority groups do not believe that the census is confidential. Those who harbor an undocumented individual in the household are especially fearful of discovery through participation in the census; others who are receiving public assistance are concerned about the government finding undeclared partners. It also seems likely that some immigrants would be wary of government initiatives to count and document individuals and skeptical about confidentiality claims because of their negative experiences with government activities in their native countries.

Limited English Proficiency

Finally, the ethnographic studies found that lack of English proficiency was a major source of undercounts in some communities. The studies made use of native-speaker enumerators who could conduct the census in Haitian creole, Spanish, Chinese, and a variety of other languages. Multilingualism proved to be enormously important, both enabling effective communication and inducing the respondent to trust the enumerator. In addition, immigrant populations are often characterized by a high incidence of illiteracy in the native tongue. Ethnographers sometimes found that members of their target population were unable to read or write in any language. Illiteracy necessitates even more intervention or interpretation in the enumeration process and undoubtedly introduces standardization problems. Coverage was undoubtedly improved in these case studies; consistency may be another matter.

Summary

It is important to remember that the Ethnographic Evaluation Project was conducted in particularly hard-to-count neighborhoods. Nonetheless, the project sheds light on the causes of undercounts and overcounts and suggests valuable policy initiatives. These initiatives need to be built into the research and implementation process for the 2000 census if the coverage issue is to be actively addressed. The intensive nature of alternative enumeration methods will make them costly, but if they are effective in addressing differential undercounts they may end up saving the Census Bureau funds that might otherwise have to be used for follow-up.

The ethnographic research makes it abundantly clear that individuals familiar with the native languages, customs, and the physical layout of the communities in question were far more successful than traditional enumerators in locating and surveying hard-to-count populations. The project directors concluded, and this panel concurs, that the Census Bureau should create a more effective partnership with locally based, grass-roots organizations in order to address the coverage problem. Some of these organizations have regional and even national representation (e.g., the Urban League, Mexican American Legal Defense Fund); others are entirely local in orientation. These two kinds of ethnic organizations appeal to different groups and would require different partnership strategies with the Census Bureau, but both must be approached and integrated into the 2000 census.

Effective partnerships between the Census Bureau and local leadership will have to be inaugurated well before census day. There is reason to believe that a continuous outreach, promotion, and enumeration operation in targeted areas will end up being cost-effective in comparison with the start-and-stop approach that has been used. Developing local ties that work--that is, that help to reduce the differential undercount by creating a participatory spirit or simply by using the superior knowledge of local "ethnographers"--is not an overnight operation. If such efforts prove effective--as they have, to some extent, for Statistics Canada with regard to the Canadian aboriginal population--they should pay off in terms of reduced undercount and more effective targeting of Census Bureau resources.

Implementing an in-depth, localized, network approach will demand an enormous change in the culture of the Census Bureau where, for perfectly understandable reasons, centralized control and standardized methods have been paramount. Involvement of community organizations at the level suggested by the ethnographic studies will mean yielding a degree of control, and fostering a sense of trust, that would probably be unparalleled in the agency's history. Community leaders speak of the importance of defining the census as "theirs," the critical need to "own" the census, rather than approaching the census as an instrument that belongs to the government or to the nation as a whole. It is important to recognize how revolutionary "going local" on this scale would be.

At the same time, the survival of many community organizations depends on the census, because their funding is linked directly to the size of the populations they serve. If for no other reason than self-interest, many Native American, Haitian, African-American, Hispanic, and Pacific Islander social service agencies are eager to help. Grass-roots groups have infrastructures that can be of enormous assistance in the enumeration process; they know where to find their people, they have lists of their members, and they are trusted in the community. These are assets that cannot be acquired by outsiders, and they are directly related to a successful enumeration. One concern with grass-roots efforts, however, is the potential for increases in erroneous enumerations and consequent overcounting when the involved organizations may be interested more in the size rather than the accuracy of the count. Procedures will require adequate safeguards to prevent problems of this nature.

> **Recommendation 3.8:** The Census Bureau should consider developing an extensive network of relations between field offices and local community resources. This infrastructure would be maintained in continuous operation between and during census years. The Census Bureau should develop and implement pilot programs in conjunction with the 1995 census test in order to gather information about the potential costs and benefits of a large-scale local outreach program.

There is a tendency to assume that irregular households are the product of culturally specific notions of family, but the evidence from the case studies suggests a surprising degree of uniformity in the residence practices of the nation's poor, whether immigrant or native-born. Further research is needed. Results must be incorporated into the targeting model and into any component of the census design that depends on comprehensive coverage (e.g., CensusPlus). A theoretical understanding of the distribution of the hard-to-enumerate population is needed, one that looks across ethnic and racial groups to the common characteristics of the poor; that theoretical knowledge is of considerable practical value in directing additional resources to field offices where differential undercounts are likely. The same modeling may help in determining the most effective placement of the standing infrastructure discussed in Recommendation 3.8 (above).

> **Recommendation 3.9:** The Census Bureau should conduct further comparative studies of hard-to-enumerate areas, focusing on those parts of the country where three phenomena coincide: a shortage of affordable housing, a high proportion of undocumented immigrants, and the presence of low-income neighborhoods.

Ethnographers believe that enumerators who reflect the racial, ethnic, and cultural composition of the target population and who are residents of the community should be hired to conduct the census collection itself. Some of the advantages are trust, communication skills (especially foreign language skills), knowledge of the housing stock, and creation of the appearance (and reality) of "local ownership" of the census. Communities that are suspicious of the federal government or that see no reward from participation are more likely to be persuaded of the importance of the census if the words come from people they know and have reason to admire or trust. One potential disadvantage with community enumerators is that respondents may be reluctant to give accurate information about more sensitive items, such as income, to a friend or neighbor.

Local enumerators are more likely to know the ins and outs of the neighborhoods that feature irregular housing, but further training and support for locating hidden housing units will be necessary. The ethnographic studies recommend making more systematic use of mail carriers, not to conduct the count, but as sources for identifying housing units. Rental offices and landlords turn out to be poor sources of information, but mail carriers are disinterested parties whose knowledge base is currently underused.

Clearly a large-scale program of "ethnic enumerators" would require a significant change in traditional training methods. More resources would have to be available to train enumerators, and the process would take longer. It would be foolhardy to hire people and provide them with insufficient training. But the investment would be well worth it if the program contributed to reducing the differential undercount--particularly if it was tied to an ongoing organizational structure (which would not have to be reborn with every decennial census).

Ethnographers working in Spanish-speaking areas noted the importance of developing Spanish-language census forms based on a conceptual rather than a literal translation and distributing these forms more effectively than in 1990, when people were required to call a toll-free number to request a Spanish-language form. They reported frustration on the part of Spanish speakers who were unable to participate even though they are literate in their native tongue. This would seem a relatively simple and cost-effective recommendation. Every form that can be completed by mail saves on the cost of follow-up. Although this was the only non-English-language form suggestion, further research on the efficacy of translating the form into other languages might be useful. Further research is needed to assess whether the use of foreign-language tapes or interactive video might be effective ways of reaching individuals who are not literate in their native language.

Immigrant families working shifts and seasonal jobs are often difficult to enumerate because their schedules are irregular. Ethnographers recommend that enumerators conduct visits in the evening and on weekends, rather than in the middle of workdays in order to find more people at home. They also noted the importance of moving the census day so that it falls in the middle of the month; occupants of low-cost housing are more likely to move at the beginning and the end of a month. Hence, a change in the timing of the census itself will reduce that part of the undercount that is attributable to residential mobility. (Statistics Canada has already changed census day for essentially the same reasons. Officials concluded that part of the undercount problem could be solved simply by moving the census date from the first day of the month. The Census Bureau should consider following suit.)

> **Recommendation 3.10:** In the 1995 census test, the Census Bureau should evaluate specific measures and procedures that might improve the enumeration of historically undercounted populations. Candidates for study in 1995 should include a larger repertoire of foreign-language materials (both written and audio), more aggressive hiring of community-based enumerators, and greater flexibility in the timing of enumeration (i.e., contact during evenings and weekends). In particular, the Census Bureau should examine the efficacy of moving census day to the middle of the month.

Ethnographers noted the increasingly outdated conceptualization of race and ethnic identity embodied in the census. America is becoming a multicultural society, and personal identities are changing alongside this trend. The selection of single-race identifiers is proving particularly problematic under these circumstances. Are immigrants supposed to define themselves by nationality, ethnicity, language group, or physical appearance? Are individuals supposed to select a category that expresses how they view themselves or how others define them? This is a source of great confusion. Laotian nationals of Chinese descent and Hmong origin do not know which way to turn. Spanish-speaking Filipinos are unsure whether they should check "Pacific Islander" for race and then "Hispanic" for origin.

The single identification items are based on a long-standing conceptualization of race (and ethnicity) as unambiguous, whereas contemporary identification is more fluid and situational. The United States is starting to look more like Brazil or Tahiti, among the many places in the world where fluid racial and ethnic identity is the norm and where single-category identifications are not easily reconciled with personal conceptions of race. As immigration patterns bring more people from these societies (e.g., the Dominican Republic) to the United States, patterns of identification are shifting. The Census Bureau needs to invest time and support in research on these questions, and policy makers need to clarify the purpose of the identification questions themselves. The Panel on Census Requirements in the Year 2000 and Beyond is currently investigating the subject of racial and ethnic classification with regard to content needs in the decennial census and other demographic programs.

These problems are not contributing to the undercount, in the sense of "missing persons," but they are at the heart of another kind of problem: ethnic and racial misclassification. The Census Bureau will continue to feel pressure to solve this problem as long as resource flows to ethnic community organizations depend on the accurate classification and counting of their members. We recognize that these are extremely difficult problems to solve, and we recommend, among other things, that the Census Bureau experiment with multiple check-off classification schemes in the 1995 census test. We further suggest that the Census Bureau sponsor additional research on the question of ethnic identity, utilizing the intellectual resources of cognitive anthropology (where much relevant research has already been done) and sociology.

> **Recommendation 3.11:** The Census Bureau should consider a major program of research in cognitive anthropology, sociology, and psychology that will comprehensively examine the issue of racial and ethnic identity. This research would contribute to the development of more acceptable racial and ethnic identification questions. In particular, the Census Bureau should consider experimenting with allowing people to select more than one race category in the 1995 test.

The policy recommendations that emerged from the ethnographic studies are of enormous value for the 2000 census. What remains to be seen is how they can be incorporated into the tool kit: it is unclear that there is any meaningful link between the two enterprises. It certainly is insufficient to list "ethnography" as part of the tool kit; the word has no content for local census officials. What must be spelled out are the strategies of outreach and enumeration that an ethnographically inspired approach would entail. For the most part, this would seem to involve localized, customized methods of recruiting enumerators drawn from minority populations, providing ongoing outreach support to their organizations, and using their greater trust and recognition within hard-to-enumerate populations as a basis for a partnership. Instructions need to go to field offices about how to find these people, particularly if they are disconnected from large and nationally known organizations (e.g., the Urban League). Training programs need to be developed, and they will take time.

It should be noted that what ethnography provides is not a set of methods for collecting the census, but a knowledge base for mapping a community and an approach for recruiting culturally knowlededgable enumerators who can do an effective job in working with hard-to-enumerate populations.

RESIDENCE RULES

Promotion, outreach, and greater flexibility in methods of enumeration will probably have their greatest effect on household coverage, *not* on coverage of people within households. We emphasize that improving coverage of persons within households--and reducing the contribution of within-household coverage to the differential undercount--requires reducing response error, because it is household respondents who implement the residence rules as they fill out the census form or talk with a Census Bureau enumerator.

Areas with large minority and renter populations, homeless persons, and children in shared custody arrangements are examples of cases that present special problems in accurately applying the Census Bureau's residence rules. The Living Situation Survey (LSS), a national household sample weighted toward minority populations, is an attempt to better understand the living situations in these groups. This survey is expected to help the Census Bureau determine the effects of complex living arrangements on coverage and residence rules. The results from the LSS and the ethnographic evaluations conducted for the 1990 census can contribute to improving the conceptualizations underlying residence rules as well as their application. Results from the LSS will probably not be available in time to directly influence current tests of new residence rules and their application, but the Census Bureau's research staff is aware of the potential contribution of the LSS, and we expect the knowledge gained from developing the LSS to have an indirect effect on the design of residence rules for the decennial census.

We understand that current plans for research on improving within-household coverage include testing a version of the residence rules in which respondents begin by listing people who have stayed in the household and then go through the steps of adding people who meet and subtracting people who do not meet residence criteria.

If the 2000 census is to use *de jure* residence rules, we think that beginning with a kind of *de facto* listing and then applying the rules systematically promises to increase the accuracy with which respondents apply the Census Bureau's rules. We also think that such an approach is more likely to minimize mode effects than the approach used in 1990.

Once again, we recognize that not all issues can be taken into account in designing such a complex project. But we recommend that two census forms--one to be self-administered and one to be administered by an interviewer over the telephone--be developed simultaneously. It is important to have this dual goal in mind while the instrument is being designed, because some features can be moved more easily from a telephone to a self-administered presentation than vice versa. The goal of simultaneous development is a self-administered questionnaire that can be given a comparable implementation for telephone. This comparability is particularly important for census residence rules. The research program would have to determine at the outset whether a census telephone interviewer would use computer-assisted telephone interviewing or a paper instrument because these could require very different designs.

Particularly if the telephone will be used for follow-up in 2000, the comparability of self-administered and telephone administered instruments must be evaluated. Such an evaluation could use experimental treatments, such as the following: (1) respondent completes a self-administered instrument, (2) respondent who is looking at a self-administered form is interviewed by telephone, and (3) respondent who is not looking at a self-administered form is interviewed by telephone. This evaluation would not necessarily require a study of the magnitude of the MTMT or the other response improvement studies. Information on the presence and size of mode effects on within-household coverage could also be important in correctly specifying the models used in mixed-mode coverage measurement methods, such as SuperCensus and CensusPlus.

The experiments to improve within-household coverage with new forms of residence rules discussed above offer an opportunity to test a form for the 1995 census test, and the Census Bureau should take full advantage of this opportunity. If possible, cognitive laboratory testing should be conducted using final versions of the instrument. It appears that the questionnaire designed in these experiments will build on the organizational experience gained in the Simplified Questionnaire Test (SQT). Research on residence rules in the LSS is also likely to extend well beyond the 1995 test. This project obviously has implications for almost any of the census designs and for other surveys.

> **Recommendation 3.12:** When developing and applying residence rules, the Census Bureau should consider both the need to accurately enumerate diverse household structures and the potential for mode effects when an instrument is implemented in both self-administered and interviewer-administered forms. In particular, the Census Bureau should simultaneously develop enumeration forms designed for self-administration and telephone administration for use in

the 1995 census test. The comparability of these forms should subsequently be evaluated on the basis of 1995 census test results.

4

ADMINISTRATIVE RECORDS:
INTRIGUING PROSPECTS, FORMIDABLE OBSTACLES

Rapid expansion of the coverage, content, and computerization of administrative records containing information about persons, families, addresses, and housing units is a fact that is receiving increased attention from both statistical agencies and data users. How and to what extent can enhanced uses of these records supplement and perhaps even replace the more traditional methods for direct collection of population and housing data? What potential exists for significantly reducing the cost of producing small-area data and obtaining data more frequently?

It would be unnecessarily limiting to look at such uses of administrative records solely within the context of the decennial census. The decennial census is part of a population and housing data system that also includes continuing and periodic sample surveys of households and persons and a program of intercensal population estimates that already makes use of several kinds of administrative records. Administrative records maintained by program agencies at all levels of government are used by the statistical units in some of those agencies to produce valuable statistical data.

So far there have been only limited uses of administrative records in the decennial censuses (private communication, Susan Miskura, 1993). For future censuses, the panel is exploring their possible uses either as the primary source of census data (as is now done in some European countries) or as a significant adjunct to traditional census methods, to improve coverage, content, or the efficiency of census operations and to evaluate census results. Both this panel and the Panel on Census Requirements have chosen to study possible uses of administrative records within a broader context. Thus, we are considering possible uses of administrative records in the 2000 census and the testing of such uses in 1995, and we are also looking at censuses beyond 2000 and at other components of the U.S. demographic data system.

We begin this chapter by summarizing prior recommendations about uses of administrative records from our panel's December 1992 letter report (Committee on National Statistics, 1992) and from the interim report of the Panel on Census Requirements (Committee on National Statistics, 1993). We then discuss the underlying policy and broad technical issues that we believe are critical to the success or failure of efforts to make more effective use of administrative records for demographic data. We review and comment on the current status of plans for using administrative records in the 2000 census and for testing such uses in 1995. We also look beyond the 2000 census toward a long-term program of research and development that could lead to a census based primarily on administrative records in 2010 or to other significant uses of administrative records for small-area population and housing data. Finally, we identify some questions about administrative records that we expect to consider and address in our final report.

PRIOR FINDINGS AND RECOMMENDATIONS

In the panel's letter report of December 14, 1992, to the director of the Census Bureau (Committee on National Statistics, 1992), we agreed with the Census Bureau's conclusion that a census based primarily on administrative records was not a feasible option for 2000 (Bureau of the Census, 1992a). A primary reason given by the Census Bureau for this conclusion was that the race and ethnicity information needed from the census to comply with requirements of the Voting Rights Act is not currently available for most persons from any single administrative records source or combination of sources. In the view of the panel, however, "The primary issues surrounding the two administrative record designs . . . are not necessarily voting rights data, but privacy, coverage, geography, and the whole range of content" (Committee on National Statistics, 1992:6)

Our panel believes that the Census Bureau should be doing more to explore emerging possibilities for expanded uses of administrative records in its demographic data programs. Specifically, the panel recommended that the Census Bureau:

• initiate a separate program of research on uses of administrative records, not directly tied to the 2000 census, focusing primarily on the 2010 census and on current estimates programs.

• undertake a planning study to develop one or more detailed design options for a 2010 administrative records census (a prospectus for such a study was included as an attachment to the panel's report);

• seek the cooperation of federal agencies that maintain key administrative record systems in undertaking a series of experimental administrative records mini-censuses, including one concurrent with the 2000 census, and related projects; and

• give priority to some use of administrative records in the 2000 census for those purposes for which such use is still feasible, such as coverage and content improvement and coverage evaluation.

The Panel on Census Requirements, in one of three formal recommendations in its interim report, specifically endorsed the above recommendations. In addition, the text of the requirements panel's interim report makes clear that that panel supports increased exploitation of administrative records for intercensal population estimates, starting immediately, both as an end in itself and as a means of gaining experience that can lead to their expanded use in the decennial census. In discussing its future activities, the requirements panel expressed the belief ". . . that it is important to examine the potential of administrative records to complement or perhaps substitute for all or part of the decennial census" (Committee on National Statistics, 1993:30). The requirements panel plans to examine operational, legal, administrative, and privacy issues related to such uses of administrative records.

Finally, in Appendix B of its interim report, the requirements panel included, without endorsement or recommendations but with an invitation for comments, a short paper, "Developing New Sources for Small-Area Data." The system described in that paper would exploit current information technology and would make extensive use of administrative records. It might eventually replace the decennial census as the main source of small-area data, providing data much more frequently than once every 10 years.

The system would use administrative records from all levels of government in three ways. Initially, records from a particular system could be used on a stand-alone basis to summarize and map data for geographic areas already identified in the system. For example, a system containing addresses with ZIP codes in its records could be used to map data to the ZIP-code level. As a second step, these same records could be linked to a geographic database to produce data at the individual block or block face level. A third step would link records from different sources at the individual address level in order to undertake analyses that would not be possible with aggregate data from each source. There would, of course, be important questions of confidentiality protection associated with each type of use, especially for linkages at the individual address level.

As an illustration of what might be done, the paper describes Statistics Canada's program that provides annual data on tax filers and sources of income, based on tax records, for relatively small areas. A recent comparison of the data from this source with the 1991 Canadian census showed that the tax records data covered 97 percent of the census population and 99 percent of the population in families (Standish et al., 1993). This particular illustration belongs in the first category described above: it does not require any linkages to a geographic database or to records from other administrative sources. Comparable U.S. studies are discussed following recommendation 4.6 (below).

BASIC REQUIREMENTS FOR MORE EFFECTIVE USE OF ADMINISTRATIVE RECORDS

The panel believes that many statistical uses of administrative records are appropriate and have important advantages. Such records can play an important part in meeting needs for basic demographic data, especially for small geographic areas. In this section we discuss major policy and technical issues that must be addressed in an effective long-range effort to develop effective uses of administrative records.

Access

Effective use of administrative records by the Census Bureau requires a legal right to access, the establishment of close and mutually beneficial ongoing relationships between the Census Bureau and the custodians of administrative records, and reasonable assurance of continued access. By a legal right to access, we mean at least the absence of legal prohibitions on access for statistical uses, and, preferably, positive statutory recognition of statistical uses as a permissible secondary use of the records. The Census Bureau probably has greater legal access to administrative records than any other U.S. statistical agency, but its access is by no means universal, especially with regard to systems maintained at the state level, for which access is controlled by state laws.

Legal access is necessary but not sufficient for effective use. Access in specific instances is often arranged only with great difficulty. These difficulties will continue unless both statistical agencies and the custodians of record systems develop new ways of thinking about statistical uses of administrative records. The custodians need to regard satisfying the statistical requirements of the nation as one of the responsibilities on which they will be judged, not as an inconvenience or an intrusion on their territory. There has to be some flexibility on the part of both statistical and program agencies in adapting their operating procedures and schedules to meet basic statistical needs. There must also be willingness by the statistical agencies to assist administrative agencies in every possible way, for example, by providing technical support to the latter for the production of small-area tabulations of administrative records, to the extent that this can be done while ensuring a one-way flow of administrative records for statistical uses.

Statistics Canada's access to administrative records, which makes possible the data system described in Appendix B of the Requirements Panel's Interim Report, may provide a useful model. For the United States, a 1976 policy statement of the Social Security Administration (U.S. Department of Health and Human Services, 1976:17) is relevant:

> The operation of the social security system produces a vast and unique body of statistical information about employment, payrolls, life-time earnings histories, retirement, disability, mortality and benefit claims and payments.

> The Social Security Administration has an obligation to develop these data according to the best scientific standards and with maximum economy and minimum delay, and to publish them in a form useful both to the program administrator and to social scientists generally. It also has an obligation to encourage the linkage of these data with other bodies of statistical information, and to make the data available for research uses by other organizations, subject always to careful safeguarding of the confidentiality of information relating to individuals.

The panel notes the Census Bureau's initiative in organizing a July 15, 1993, Interagency Conference on Statistical Uses of Administrative Records and its plan to hold a similar meeting involving custodians of state record systems. We urge the participants to take advantage of this beginning by moving to establish a regular mechanism for closer collaboration between custodians and users of administrative records.

Effective use of Internal Revenue Service (IRS) records in the decennial census and other Census Bureau programs requires a close working relationship between the two agencies. In the past, the two agencies have sometimes had difficulty in agreeing on their respective roles and in developing and maintaining smooth working arrangements. Given the importance of these programs to the entire federal statistical system, these difficulties suggest a need for involvement by the Statistical Policy Office of the Office of Management and Budget (OMB).

The Census Bureau can only commit itself to substantially greater reliance on administrative records if it can have reasonable assurance of continued access. As an illustration of the type of problem that can occur, Standish et al. (1993) note that, as a result of changes in Canada's system of family allowances, some of the information about children that had been used in the statistical program (described above) will no longer be available. It is also important that proposed legislation requiring the establishment of major new administrative records systems be carefully monitored to ensure that possibilities for important statistical uses of the records are recognized and are not unnecessarily foreclosed. New systems established in connection with health care reform might offer a less controversial alternative to other major federal record systems as a primary source of population data.

> **Recommendation 4.1:** The Statistical Policy Office in the Office of Management and Budget should recognize statistical uses of administrative records as one of its major areas of responsibility and should assume an active role in facilitating more effective working relationships between statistical and program agencies and in tracking relevant legislation.

Public Acceptance

No plan for expanded statistical uses of administrative records can succeed unless it has the acceptance of the people who provide the data to the program agencies. Greater use of administrative records could reduce the number of separate occasions on which individuals are asked to provide information about themselves to the government, and it also has the potential for substantially reducing the cost of censuses. The key issues, however, are consent and confidentiality. Do people accept the use of information about themselves for statistical purposes that are not directly related to the purposes for which they supplied the information? Should they be able, as individuals, to prevent such uses? Will the confidentiality of their data be adequately protected? Effective use of administrative records for census evaluation, coverage improvement, and supplementation of content may require that identifiers--such as full name, date of birth or Social Security number--be collected in the census and entered into census electronic files, along with addresses. Will this be acceptable? These are not easy questions. We note that many of them have been explored in the report of the Panel on Confidentiality and Data Access (Duncan et al., 1993).

The panel believes that it is necessary to proceed with public debate about the ethical, legal, and policy issues associated with statistical uses of administrative records. The Census Bureau has had numerous contacts with privacy advocates in connection with previous censuses and has informed the panel that it plans future discussions that will focus specifically on statistical uses of administrative records. However, there has been a tendency on the part of the agencies involved to back away from a public debate for fear that calling attention to these questions might lead to discontinuance of important existing activities, such as the use of tax return and Social Security data in the Census Bureau's intercensal population estimates programs. We believe it is time to face these questions directly. Such a debate is likely to be more productive if it focuses on specific uses of administrative records, such as the implications of an administrative records census in 2010, rather than on broad philosophical questions.

Surveys and focus group interviews can help provide background for public discussions of these issues. Some information on taxpayers' opinions about possible uses of their data in the census of population and for other statistical purposes was collected in a survey conducted for the IRS, the 1990 Taxpayer Opinion Survey. Neither the report nor the planned public-use microdata files from that survey have yet been released. When they are, the panel expects to analyze the data for information about the public's views on these issues.

Recommendation 4.2: The Census Bureau should initiate a systematic process of consultation and research to explore the attitudes of the public, political representatives, and other opinion leaders about the use of administrative records as an integral part of the census. Previous consultations and existing research, such as the yet-to-be-released 1990 Taxpayer Opinion Survey, should be taken into account.

Technical Requirements

Several of the central themes that are discussed in Chapter 1--including address list development, record linkage research, the need for long-term planning and the need for greater interagency cooperation and coordination--are critical to making better use of administrative records in the decennial census and for other programs to produce small-area population and housing data. The first two of these are technical requirements, and in this subsection we discuss briefly their particular relevance to the use of administrative records.

As stated in Chapter 1, the panel believes that a geographic database that is fully integrated with a master address file is a basic requirement, whether for a traditional census or for one making greater use of administrative records. To be cost-effective and available for noncensus uses, the system should be continuously updated. Its coverage should be extended to rural areas, and conversion of rural-type addresses to street addresses should be promoted by all means possible. Appendix B to the interim report of the Panel on Census Requirements explains clearly how such a system could serve as the keystone for using administrative records data to provide small-area data more frequently and inexpensively. We recommend (Recommendation 1.1) that the transition to a continuous, integrated system begin now, at least for the areas in which the 1995 census test is to be conducted, so that it can receive its first major tryout in the 1995 test.

Record linkage--that is, the identification of records belonging to the same unit, either within a single data set or in two different data sets--is critical to enhanced uses of administrative records, whether in the context of a full administrative records census or a more traditional design. If different administrative data sets are to be used to improve the coverage of the master address file or of persons at known addresses, duplicates must be identified and eliminated. Uses of administrative records to supply missing data or to evaluate the coverage and content of the census enumeration all require some type of record linkage for persons or addresses.

Record linkage, like any element of census data collection and processing, is subject to error. The Census Bureau and other organizations have developed effective techniques for linking large data sets, but many aspects need further research and development as the techniques are applied in specific circumstances. How can the inputs be standardized to facilitate linkages? Over how wide an area should initial computerized matches be undertaken? What are the best keys (e.g., name, address, date of birth, or Social Security number), alone or in combination, and what are the costs and other considerations for capturing these items in the computerized files for a census or evaluation survey? Additional research on these questions is a prerequisite to success in making more effective use of administrative records. Testing should be carried out in conjunction with the 2000 census and the tests leading up to it and also in separate initiatives to explore the possibility of a 2010 census based primarily on administrative records.

Another technical requirement for enhanced uses of administrative records is knowledge about the quality of the data that they can provide. How well do administrative record systems, individually or in combination, cover the target population for a census? Recent work in the United States (Sailer et al., 1993) and in Canada (Standish et al., 1992) indicates that well over 90 percent of the respective countries' enumerated populations can be identified in their tax systems, not supplemented by any other source. How much could this coverage be improved by adding records from other systems, and how would the coverage of subgroups defined by geography or other characteristics (differential coverage) be affected, both in absolute and relative terms?

Besides coverage, the accuracy and relevance of data available from administrative records need to be considered. For example, suppose there are administrative data for persons whose census responses are incomplete. Is enough known about the quality of these data to make an informed choice among alternatives: further nonresponse follow-up, imputation based on similar persons, or substitution of the administrative data? To what extent could tax data be used either to evaluate or substitute for income data collected in a census? What are the implications of conceptual differences? Opportunities and resources should be sought to pursue questions like these.

USE OF ADMINISTRATIVE RECORDS IN THE 2000 CENSUS

During the remainder of this decade, the primary goals for expanded uses of administrative records should be: to experiment in the 1995 census test with the uses considered most promising for the 2000 census and, based on the results, to make appropriate uses of administrative records in the 2000 census; and to begin an active continuing program of research and development for a possible 2010 census based primarily on administrative records and for other uses of records in demographic data programs. These two streams of activity should proceed in parallel, and they must be carefully coordinated. Uses of administrative records in the 2000 census are discussed in this section. The following section presents our views on research and development that focuses on the 2010 census and other uses.

In our earlier letter report, we accepted the Census Bureau's judgment that an administrative records census would not be possible for 2000, but we recommended that the Census Bureau give priority to some uses of administrative records in the 2000 census for purposes for which such use is demonstrated to be feasible. Possible uses in the census can be classified into four broad groups:

(1) *Measures to improve coverage.* Coverage improvement measures divide into those aimed at improving the master address file and those aimed at improving the coverage of individuals. The former can be used throughout the decade, or at least prior to the census, to ensure a good starting address list. The latter need to use records current at the time of the census and will tend to focus on administrative sources that are rich in data on difficult-to-enumerate subpopulations. Both kinds of uses of administrative records could be made across the board or for a sample of blocks as part of a built-in adjustment process designed to produce a one-number census. Administrative records would be a logical element of a CensusPlus or SuperCensus design (see Chapter 2) in which close to 100 percent coverage is sought for a sample of areas, or they could serve as one of the sources in a dual- or triple-system estimation design.

(2) *Measures to improve content.* Administrative records have already been used to some extent for evaluation purposes--for example, in record checks with tax data to assess income reporting. A next step could be to use them as a source of data to replace data that are missing due to nonresponse or data that failed edit tests. The

final level would be to use administrative records as the initial source of data for some variables, with some form of follow-up for missing data cases as necessary.

(3) *Measures to improve operational efficiency.* The use of administrative records as a source of telephone numbers is one example of use for operational efficiency. Administrative records data could be used prior to the census to identify hard-to-enumerate areas for which special enumeration methods might be appropriate.

(4) *Measures to evaluate the census.* Uses of administrative records for evaluation will depend very much on how the 2000 census methodology develops with regard to integrated coverage processes that are designed as part of a one-number census. To the extent that administrative records are not used to improve content, they could be used to evaluate content.

It is now clear that the 1995 census test will not be a test of one or more of the 14 designs proposed at the beginning of the selection process; rather, it will be a test of features taken from several of the 14 designs. Many of the features selected for testing will represent significant changes from the 1990 design. Although informal discussions have identified some of the features that are receiving strong consideration, the Census Bureau has not yet released a detailed proposal identifying and describing the uses of administrative records that it proposes to test.

Rather than recommend specific features for testing, the panel wishes at this time to make three broad recommendations concerning uses of administrative records in the 1995 census test. We assume that the 1995 test sites will include both urban and rural areas and that they will be determined in fall 1993, with enumeration in the spring of 1995.

> **Recommendation 4.3:** As part of the 1995 census test, the Census Bureau should construct an administrative records database for the test sites.

The administrative records database for the 1995 census test should be designed to serve two objectives: (1) testing uses of administrative records that appear to be promising for the 2000 census, and (2) obtaining information, especially about the population coverage of major administrative record systems, that will be useful in exploring the feasibility of a census based primarily on administrative records in 2010 (for more discussion of this goal, see the following section). In order to serve both purposes, the database for the 1995 test sites should include address and person information extracted from both federal and local record systems. Federal systems, particularly those of the IRS and Social Security Administration, are known to cover a large proportion of the total population.

If the Census Bureau fails to take advantage of the 1995 test to start exploring the possibilities of a census based largely on administrative records in 2010, there will be a danger of repeating the pattern of the current and earlier decennial census cycles, in which consideration of the administrative records option was begun too late to make it a serious contender for the subsequent census.

Recommendation 4.4: The Census Bureau should establish the testing of record linkage procedures as an important goal of the 1995 census test.

For this purpose, it will be necessary to collect and capture electronically one or more of four potential matching keys: full name, date of birth, address, and Social Security number. Address and either name or birth date should be captured for all persons enumerated, and all four keys should be captured for a sample of persons (with the Social Security number being treated as a voluntary item), so that their relative effectiveness as matching keys can be evaluated. The provision of Social Security number should be clearly identified as voluntary on questionnaires and in follow-up interviews.

Recommendation 4.5: In preparation for uses of administrative records in the 1995 census test, detailed negotiations between the Census Bureau and the other relevant agencies should begin immediately, with the involvement of the Statistical Policy Office of the Office of Management and Budget (see also Recommendation 4.1).

In addition to the content and delivery dates of records to be made accessible to the Census Bureau, the negotiations could cover possible modifications to standard administrative record formats for the test areas during the relevant periods and tabulations that the other agencies might make of their own records for comparative evaluation purposes.

USE OF ADMINISTRATIVE RECORDS IN 2010 AND BEYOND

A successful long-range effort to define and develop new uses of administrative records for demographic data requires a strategic plan, embracing a full array of censuses, current surveys, population estimates, and small-area data from program records as a system. Such a plan cannot succeed if it is developed unilaterally by the Census Bureau. Within the federal statistical community, planning must involve other statistical agencies and OMB's Statistical Policy Office. A broad range of data users must be consulted, and the custodians of major administrative record systems must be actively involved.

As detailed above, the panel recommended in its letter report that the Census Bureau initiate a separate program of research on uses of administrative records, focusing primarily on the 2010 census and on current estimates programs (Committee on National Statistics, 1992). It also recommended a planning study to develop one or more detailed design options for a 2010 administrative records census and initiation of a series of administrative records mini-censuses.

The Census Bureau has indicated its intentions to start these activities in fiscal 1995 if resources permit. The panel believes that an earlier start would be desirable so that the needs of the long-range program can be taken into account in planning for the 1995 census test. The 1995 census test and the 2000 census will provide valuable opportunities to gain experience that will facilitate uses of administrative records in a 2010 census and in other programs. Once prototype designs have been developed for a 2010 administrative records census--an objective of the "HOW Study" that we recommended (Committee on National Statistics, 1992)--the following type of development program can be envisioned:

(1) pilot test(s) to construct a census purely from administrative records in a defined and limited geographic area--primarily to learn of the problems;

(2) test(s) as in (1), but in conjunction with a conventional census test to allow evaluation of coverage;

(3) test(s) that incorporate follow-up activities to investigate missing addresses and households for which the administrative data fail to meet standards for completeness and consistency--primarily procedural tests;

(4) test(s) as in (3), but in conjunction with a conventional census test to allow evaluation of coverage (which will require careful design to ensure that the administrative records test and the conventional census do not affect each other);

(5) full stand-alone dress rehearsal(s) of an administrative records census in chosen areas, using the procedures found to be most effective in steps (1) to (4).

The 1995 census test would present the first opportunity for a type (2) test. Tests of types (3), (4) and (5) could be undertaken in conjunction with the final tests for the 2000 census and the census itself. The main point we wish to make here is that, in planning for the 2000 census, the Census Bureau should make a serious effort to incorporate testing of possible administrative records uses for the 2010 census and other purposes.

The 1950 decennial census provides a model for this kind of long-range planning and experimentation. Self-enumeration, which was extended to most of the country in 1960, was tested in experimental areas in the 1950 census. The 1950 census also saw the first use of an electronic computer (UNIVAC I) for data processing on a limited basis; by 1960 most of the processing was done on computers (Goldfield, 1992). In planning for future uses of administrative records, it is necessary to break out of the 10-year planning cycle that always looks only to the next census. If this does not happen, intriguing prospects will not become real gains.

The Census Bureau staff that have been assigned to explore administrative records uses have displayed imagination and competence. Much has been learned about the characteristics of administrative record systems in both the public and private sectors, and this information is being systematically documented in the Census Bureau's Administrative Record Information System. These accomplishments hold promise for the future, provided the two-stream approach (described above) for the 2000 census is adopted and sufficient resources are committed soon to a serious ongoing development program.

Recommendation 4.6: The Census Bureau should establish a formal program of long-range research and development activities relating to expanded use of administrative records for demographic data.

As recommended by the Panel on Census Requirements (Committee on National Statistics, 1993), uses of administrative records in the current population estimates program should be a part of this effort.

Recent research by the Statistics of Income Division of the Internal Revenue Service has produced an estimate of 1990 U.S. population by combining data from income tax returns and information documents. The IRS estimate was equal to 98.7 percent of the unadjusted 1990 census count and 97.1 percent of the adjusted count. (The 95 percent confidence interval for the latter percent is from 96.2 percent to 98.0 percent.) State estimates exceeded 92 percent of the adjusted census counts for all but six states (Sailer et al., 1993).

Although one should not make too much of these promising but preliminary results, they do suggest the possibility that data from IRS and Social Security Administration (SSA) record systems can potentially play a much greater role than they do now in providing population counts or estimates, with some information on demographic and economic variables. The data from the IRS/SSA systems could be an important component of improved current population estimates, of a continuous measurement system, as envisaged in Design Alternative Recommendation (DAR) #14 (Bureau of the Census, 1993b) and the prototype described by Alexander (1993), and of new small-area data systems as described in Appendix B of the requirements panel's report (Committee on National Statistics, 1993).

Ideally, these possibilities should be explored jointly, with close collaboration at all stages, by the Census Bureau, the IRS and the Social Security Administration. Until now, however, the IRS's research on the development of population counts has been undertaken by the Statistics of Income Division with little input from the Census Bureau. The Statistics of Income Division has limited resources for this kind of research. Under the assumption that the Census Bureau will succeed in obtaining the resources for long-range research and development referred to in Recommendation 4.6 (above), we suggest that the Census Bureau consider the possibility of using some of these resources to fund contract work by IRS on statistical uses of IRS/SSA records. The objectives of such work would be specified in the context of the long-term needs of federal demographic data programs, with emphasis on further exploration of potential statistical uses of annual files that integrate data from tax returns and information documents. The methods and approaches to be pursued at this time would be left largely to the discretion and ingenuity of IRS. Full documentation and wide availability of the results would be important requirements for this work. We hope that the Statistical Policy Office in OMB could play an active role in facilitating this kind of interagency cooperation.

In our judgment, the successful development of IRS and SSA records for demographic data purposes depends on those organizations' having a recognized and explicit role in a cooperative process. The above approach would represent a first step in this direction. We think there is a substantial likelihood that the results of such contract work would be so promising as to make the value of these data sources for federal demographic data systems self-evident. If that does occur, we believe that any legislative, organizational, or changes needed for such uses can be addressed.

The panel is mindful of the difficulties that confront efforts to use administrative records more effectively. Public acceptance is critical. A wider understanding of the difference between statistical and nonstatistical uses of records is essential, and people must be convinced that the confidentiality of records used for statistical purposes will be fully protected. We hope to have available soon the database from the 1990 Taxpayer Opinion Survey so that we can improve our understanding of these issues. Content and user requirements for small-area data are also primary considerations. The lack of consistent and complete race and ethnicity information in administrative records systems is a special problem and one to which we plan to give further attention. We urge the Panel on Census Requirements to seek a clearer picture of what kinds of data are essential for very small areas and therefore cannot be provided by large sample surveys.

The nation's demographic data programs cannot commit to reliance on administrative records as a primary or major source of data unless continued and timely access to the key administrative data sets is assured. Access requires both clear legal authority and broad agreement throughout the executive and legislative branches of the government on the desirability of using the records for statistical purposes. As indicated in the chapter title, these are formidable obstacles. But we believe the potential benefits--in terms of data that are of equal or better quality, cost less, and are available more frequently--are great. The possibilities should be thoroughly explored, and methods sought to overcome the obstacles.

5

CONTINUOUS MEASUREMENT

Following the early work of Kish (e.g., 1981), there have been several proposals in recent years to extend the collection of census data throughout the decade, rather than restricting it to once every 10 years. Herriott et al. (1989), Horvitz (1986), and Kish (1990) have proposed various data collection schemes that involve this key concept of extending the collection of census data in a more or less continuous fashion. More recently, Alexander (1993) has put forth a relatively detailed proposal for incorporating continuous measurement as part of the 2000 census, and we discuss this proposal below. There are two essential features of the continuous measurement proposals for census data that have been made to date:

(1) virtually continuous data collection operations instead of starting and stopping every 10 years, with ensuing benefits for data quality including maintenance of a permanent enumeration staff and improvement through constant experience; and
(2) an increased frequency of available census data at all points throughout the decade (except for the smallest geographic units for which census data are produced, which might be updated once every 10 years).

In its Design Alternative Recommendation (DAR) #14, the Census Bureau indicates a commitment to fully investigating the feasibility of introducing a continuous measurement program in conjunction with the 2000 census (Bureau of the Census, 1993b:6):

We are fully committed to designing a program which would produce data continuously throughout the decade. Collecting data with such a program would be a fundamental departure from collecting "long form" data from a sample as an integral part of the decennial census. By definition, however, the 1995 Census Test, which is a one-time data collection activity, cannot explicitly address this option. The Census Test will enable us to develop accurate and cost-effective methods for the "year zero" portion of a continuous measurement system.

The panel is encouraged that the Census Bureau plans very serious consideration of the implementation of a continuous measurement program. We believe that this radically different approach to the way in which census data are viewed and collected is worthy of serious investigation, by the Census Bureau and others. We also understand the reasons why that option is not part of the 1995 census test. We do note, however, that in order for continuous measurement to be a realistic option for the 2000 census, a major effort will be required to evaluate continuous measurement options in parallel with work on the 1995 census test.

Since continuous measurement will not be part of the 1995 census test, and because the Census Bureau is still relatively early in its development of a continuous measurement program, the panel has relatively little in the way of recommendations to include in this interim report. We do anticipate having considerable discussion of this approach in our final report. Nevertheless, in view of the interesting possibilities of this option, its radically different approach to census data collection and reporting, and the need to move ahead with planning, we do offer some comments and suggestions based on current developments for continuous measurement.

> **Recommendation 5.1:** The Census Bureau should continue to explore the feasibility of a continuous measurement component to the 2000 census.

FEATURES AND GOALS OF CONTINUOUS MEASUREMENT

Although a number of variants of continuous measurement have already been proposed, and no doubt many more can and will be proposed in the future, there is one fundamental dichotomy among these proposed methods: whether continuous measurement is a replacement for or a supplement to a decennial population count. Kish (1990), for example, writing for an international audience, has proposed a "rolling census" in which there would be no complete enumeration of the population decennially. The Census Bureau's Design Alternative Recommendations (DARs) are clearly based on the presumption that there will be a population enumeration in 2000 and that continuous measurement would substitute only for content not needed for purposes of reapportionment and redistricting. This presumption derives from the view that it is unconstitutional to eliminate the decennial enumeration (and, thus, that a rolling census such as that proposed by Kish could not replace the U.S. decennial census under the prevailing legal view). Since we lack the expertise to evaluate this legal view, we do not challenge the requirement that a continuous measurement program must be designed in conjunction with a decennial enumeration. A legal review prepared by the Congressional Research Service (Lee, 1993) and subsequent work commissioned by the Panel on Census Requirements (see Committee on National Statistics, 1993) also support the position that a decennial enumeration must accompany any program for continuous data collection.

This conclusion does have important implications for the merits of the continuous measurement option, however. Specifically, it seems very unlikely that any continuous measurement program would be less expensive than the alternative of collecting all census data at the time of the enumeration. Rather, the most likely benefits of continuous measurement would be improved quality and timeliness for various aspects of enumeration and increased frequency of data collection. (These potential benefits are discussed in the section below on potential benefits of continuous measurement.) Timeliness refers to the efficiency with which data are collected, processed, and made available to users; frequency refers to the periodicity of summary information from data collection activities. We find this a useful distinction to maintain in our discussion. The panel believes that the Census Bureau needs to establish a research program to determine whether the benefits of continuous measurement will outweigh its costs.

Because a continuous measurement program involves many highly interrelated components, it seems necessary to begin a consideration and evaluation of continuous measurement from some realistic and concrete starting point. The panel believes that the prototype by Alexander (1993) provides a very useful starting point for evaluating continuous measurement.

Alexander identifies five component features and four goals of continuous measurement. The five features are:

(1) continuous improvement frame construction, using a continuously updated master address file to build a structured list of addresses from which survey samples can be drawn;

(2) an intercensal long-form survey, based on monthly household surveys, which will produce 5-year moving averages for census tracts and 1-year moving averages for larger geographic areas;

(3) an integrated estimates program, which produces population counts at large-area and small-area levels, and works toward integrating administrative records sources into the production of these estimates;

(4) a general purpose frame, which is an enhanced continuous improvement frame created after the first decennial enumeration, for use by federal household surveys; and

(5) drastic reduction in 2000 census content (to be replaced by intercensal long-form data and estimates).

The goals identified by Alexander are:

(1) to improve the quality of the enumeration of the 2000 census, by eliminating the distraction and burden of collecting content data;

(2) to produce small-area data with sampling error comparable to 1990 long-form data, but to make these estimates more frequently than once per decade;

(3) to provide a platform for integrating data from the decennial census, household surveys, demographic estimates, the TIGER system, and administrative records, thereby eliminating duplication of effort; and

(4) to take advantage of the continuous nature of the process in order to allow continuous improvements in the quality of operations, make more effective use of experienced staff, and efficiently share data collection resources across different programs.

The panel endorses the proposal that efforts be made to integrate census operations into the Census Bureau's full spectrum of household data collection activities. We also endorse the goals laid out by Alexander. We believe that the Census Bureau's next steps should be to carry out a systematic program of research to determine the extent to which these goals are achievable.

> **Recommendation 5.2:** The Census Bureau should establish a formal set of goals for a continuous measurement program. The Census Bureau should then establish a research plan to determine the extent to which those goals are achievable.

Alexander's prototype calls for a sample of 250,000 housing units per month, to be contacted initially by mail. For a 50 percent subsample of the nonrespondents to the mail survey, a follow-up by telephone would be attempted. Of those in this subsample for whom no telephone contact could be established, a further 50 percent would be subsampled for a personal visit interview. This use of multiple modes of data collection is aimed at achieving the necessary level of response with efficient use of resources.

Because the primary response mode in Alexander's prototype would be by mail, it would not be possible to integrate the continuous collection of census data with other household surveys conducted by the Census Bureau. Those surveys are invariably too complex to conduct by mail, while the use of mail to collect census data is undoubtedly a necessity on cost grounds. However, the continuous measurement program would result in direct benefits and cost savings for household surveys by providing a continuously updated, high-quality frame, the first feature of Alexander's prototype. Under the prototype specifications for the integrated long-form monthly household surveys, the sample sizes of 1-year and 5-year cumulations would be 3 million and 15 million housing units, respectively. By comparison, the size of the long-form sample from the 1990 census is approximately 17 million housing units.

POTENTIAL BENEFITS OF CONTINUOUS MEASUREMENT

The use of a continuous measurement program in conjunction with a decennial enumeration of the entire population would have several major indirect benefits for the enumeration itself. The first is that the continuous updating of a master address file would be automatically and systematically undertaken. This in turn would have benefits for two key aspects of the count--coverage and cost. An address file that is continuously updated accrues the benefits of having trained staff, one of whose primary functions is continually to seek improvements in the procedures for updating the file. Thus, not only will the address list for the enumeration have updated data, it will be an updated product with improved data management procedures. Consequently, there should be fewer missed dwellings in the mail component of the enumeration and fewer erroneous address inclusions--which, in turn, will reduce the cost of following up mail nonresponse and decrease the level of undercoverage due to missed dwellings.

The second benefit for the enumeration is the elimination of long-form data. (Also, in the decennial year, perhaps some data that in the preceding census were short-form data and were collected from every household will instead be gathered in continuing surveys, needed from only a large subsample of households.) By restricting data collection at the time of the count to just a few data items, there will be less burden on households to complete the portion of the census that is associated with the enumeration. This reduced respondent burden is likely to lead to a modest increase in mail response rates and should make it easier to collect data during nonresponse follow-up. These factors will consequently reduce costs of the enumeration (in addition to the fact that, with no long-form data, less data will need to be processed as part of the enumeration). By concentrating census operations in the decennial year on the task of enumerating the population, it may be possible to devote greater and more diverse efforts to the task of reducing undercoverage.

The primary source of improved data quality resulting from a continuous measurement process would be an increased frequency of census data, especially for larger geographic areas. The Alexander (1993) prototype includes annual updates for larger geographic areas (such as individual states and metropolitan areas) and updates every 5 years for small areas, such as block groups, the units for which long-form data has been available in recent censuses. This contrasts with a once-a-decade census, for which data at all levels become increasingly out-of-date as each decade progresses. Early in the decade, planning and decisions are often made using data from the preceding census, which are as much as 13 years old. For many characteristics in society, these data are of very limited usefulness since they bear little resemblance to the current situation in many geographic areas.

Although it is obvious that access to more frequent data at a variety of geographic levels is highly desirable, it will come at some cost. A critical element in determining whether a continuous measurement process is appropriate and what exact form it should take will be the assessment of the tradeoff of the benefits of increased frequency of census data over time versus the increased cost that will likely ensue from collecting data continuously. Such an assessment will need to consider how quickly the relative distributions of census long-form variables change at various geographic levels.

Recommendation 5.3: The Census Bureau should undertake an extensive and systematic evaluation of the benefits from having more frequent census data available for both large and small geographic areas.

One example of the use of census data where infrequency has negative effects is in the distribution of funds for education under Chapter 1 of the Elementary and

Secondary Education Act. The formula for distributing these funds requires estimates of the number of children in poverty at the school district level. There are about 15,000 public school districts in the United States, varying greatly in size of population covered, from a few hundred to several million. Clearly such data become dated very rapidly after a decennial census, resulting over time in less equitable allocation of what are substantial Chapter 1 funds. A quantitative evaluation of the effects for the Chapter 1 program of more timely medium- and small-area estimates of the numbers of children in poverty might be an important component of an evaluation of the benefits of continuous measurement.

A second likely benefit from a continuous measurement program is improved quality of operations and, hence, of the data. By having a permanent professional census team, rather than making a special effort to mount the resources to conduct a census once a decade, improvements in the quality of census operations are likely to occur and to be maintained much more effectively. Put another way, a continuous process leads naturally to the important development of a permanent infrastructure incorporating a strong institutional memory of the entire census process. Such an ongoing commitment on the part of a census staff is also consistent with the recommendation in Chapter 3 that the Census Bureau maintain an ongoing presence in hard-to-enumerate communities, with a view to reducing differential undercount.

A third benefit is that a continuous measurement operation would appear to provide an environment more conducive to introducing data from administrative record sources as part of census data. Alexander (1993) includes this point in his integrated estimates program. Investigation and incorporation of administrative sources of data would be an ongoing initiative. A further benefit that the panel sees is that it would be possible to incorporate periodic checks of the reliability of administrative data. One of the weaknesses of such data is that changes in administrative systems over time can lead to undetected bias being introduced into the series of estimates.

By combining a continuous measurement program with a decennial enumeration, it appears likely that the accuracy of estimates could be improved by using the decennial data to augment the data from the continuous component. The relationship between the decennial short-form data and the continuous measurement data would need to be continuously reevaluated, at least implicitly through the estimation and error estimation procedures, if not explicitly as well. The gains from such an approach might make it feasible to release more timely estimates for certain areas, because smaller samples would be needed to produce reliable estimates. At least, this could be done early in a decade when the relationship between the two data sources remains strong.

Finally, a continuous measurement procedure, through the continuous updating of a master address file, would provide a quality frame for the Census Bureau's household surveys program. This should result in substantial cost savings across the full range of these surveys, thus adding to the attractiveness of the option. It should also lead to improvements in the quality of data from these surveys by reducing coverage error.

TIMING AND IMPLEMENTATION

Since continuous measurement is a very different way of approaching the collection of census content, the panel recognizes that introduction of such a program would likely be viewed with some skepticism and misgiving. Users of census data, and those responsible for paying for that information, will need to be convinced that continuous measurement has real benefits, even if the Census Bureau's research activities indicate strongly that this is the case. We believe that the Census Bureau is aware of this skepticism.

Because of the response that would probably greet the introduction of continuous measurement, the panel believes that it would be unwise to plan its introduction right after the decennial census enumeration. At that point, the stakes would be very high, since no long-form data would have been collected as part of the enumeration under the approach discussed here. Any growing pains of the continuous measurement program would receive microscopic attention at that time, with heightened concern that the program might fail to deliver fully as advertised. This would also be a time of intense activity for census operations as the enumeration procedures are completed, and efforts to complete a successful enumeration with less undercount than in previous censuses would understandably be paramount in the attention of management at that time. Therefore, we believe that the successful introduction of a continuous measurement program in conjunction with any decennial census, whether it be for 2000 or later, must take place several years prior to a census year. At such time, data users stand to gain something they would not otherwise have--timely estimates late in the decade--and the program would have the opportunity to prove its worth by the time of the enumeration, thus substantially reducing concerns about the lack of long-form data collection in conjunction with the enumeration.

> **Recommendation 5.4:** The goals for a continuous measurement program (see Recommendation 5.2) should include phasing in the continuous measurement program during the latter half of the decade prior to the relevant census year.

One particular aspect of a continuous measurement program that needs to be addressed before such a program could be implemented is that of incorporating changes in the collection instrument over time. There are two types of such changes. The first is the addition of new data items and correspondingly the deletion of those no longer deemed relevant. The second is changes in question wording or form design in order to incorporate improvements in data collection methodology. As mentioned, administrative record data might come to replace data obtained from the household sample. Changes in mode effects can also occur without any changes in the form if, for example, there is a decrease in the proportion of the population (or of particular subgroups) who return the form by mail, resulting in a greater proportion (or different portion) of the data being obtained by telephone.

Even for decennial censuses, introducing changes between one census and the next is difficult, because users expect to be able to make comparisons of data over time. This becomes a much greater issue in the case of continuous measurement, because all estimates produced consist of cumulations of at least several months of data. However, for larger geographic areas, the continuous measurement system will provide much more useful time series of annual estimates, another benefit of the more timely data provided by this approach.

Periodic household survey programs must also deal with the problem of providing reliable time-series data in the face of innovations in data collection. In general, survey programs are not critically dependent on cumulations, as an integrated estimates program would be. There are procedures for handling such changes in periodic household surveys: these procedures involve using both forms of instrument for a period of time, thus allowing users to evaluate the effects of the change on the series. For continuous measurement, this approach would likely add to the cost, since such split panels generally have to have more than half of the usual sample size in each part. Also, taking account of changes in estimates resulting from a form change might be more difficult for cumulations than it is for time series.

Recommendation 5.5: As part of its research into the feasibility of and methods for implementing a continuous measurement program, the Census Bureau should undertake a thorough study of the consequences of changes in the instrument over time, as well as changes in mode effects. A plan must be established for incorporating the effects of such changes into the cumulated estimates and into the time series produced by the continuous measurement program.

The panel is encouraged by the approach that the Census Bureau is taking to the consideration of continuous measurement, but we wish to make clear that the panel is not yet endorsing or proposing the adoption of continuous measurement as part of the 2000 census. There is substantial research and analysis that must be carried out before it is clear whether such an approach is a good one. We do think it is a real possibility, however, and we look forward to the results of the Census Bureau's evaluation activities.

REFERENCES

Alexander, Charles H.
    1993   A Prototype Design for Continuous Measurement. Demographic
            Statistical Methods Division, Bureau of the Census, U.S. Department
            of Commerce.

Bates, Nancy, and D.C. Whitford
    1991   Reaching Everyone: Encouraging Participation in the 1990 Census.
            Paper presented at the 1991 annual meetings of the American Statistical
            Association, Atlanta, Georgia. Bureau of the Census, U.S. Department
            of Commerce.

Bradburn, Norman M.
    1993   Alternative Census Methods. Written testimony of Norman Bradburn,
            chair of the Panel to Evaluate Alternative Census Methods, Committee
            on National Statistics, National Research Council. Presented before the
            Subcommittee on Census, Statistics and Postal Personnel, Committee
            on Post Office and Civil Service, U.S. House of Representatives,
            March 2.

Brownrigg, Leslie A.
    1991   Irregular Housing and the Differential Undercount of Minorities. Paper
            prepared for the Census Advisory Committee Meetings at Alexandria,
            Virginia, November 13-15, 1991. Bureau of the Census, U.S.
            Department of Commerce.

Bryant, Barbara E.
    1992   Results of the March Simplified Questionnaire Tests and Other Census
            2000 Issues. Written testimony before the Subcommittee on Census
            and Population, House Committee on Post Office and Civil Service,
            July 1. Bureau of the Census, U.S. Department of Commerce.
    1993   Decision of the director of the Bureau of the Census on whether to use
            information from the 1990 post-enumeration survey (PES) to adjust the
            base for the intercensal population estimates produced by the Bureau of
            the Census. *Federal Register* 58(1):69-78.

Bureau of the Census
    1965   *Sampling Applications in Censuses of Population and Housing.*
            Technical Paper 13, Bureau of the Census. Washington, D.C.: U.S.
            Department of Commerce.
    1992a   Administrative Records and Design Alternatives for the 2000 Census.
            Design Alternative Recommendation (DAR) #2, Year 2000 Research

and Development Staff (September). Bureau of the Census, U.S. Department of Commerce.

1992b   Assessment of Accuracy of Adjusted Versus Unadjusted 1990 Census Base for Use in Intercensal Estimates. Report of the Committee on Adjustment of Postcensal Estimates (August 7, 1992). Bureau of the Census, U.S. Department of Commerce.

1992c   Draft option paper, "USPS Involvement in the 2000 Census." Prepared by the Bureau of the Census for the Appropriations Committee, U.S. House of Representatives. U.S. Department of Commerce.

1992d   Implementation Test (IT) Mail Response Evaluation Preliminary Report. Prepared by Census Data Quality Branch, Decennial Statistical Studies Division (December). Bureau of the Census, U.S. Department of Commerce.

1992e   Master Address File: Documentation of Requirements. Paper prepared by the MAF Requirements Process Action Team (July 1, 1991). Bureau of the Census, U.S. Department of Commerce.

1992f   1990 Census Cost Components. Year 2000 Research and Development staff memorandum series, Book I, Chapter 30, No. 4. Memo from Jay Keller to Susan Miskura (August 6, 1992). Bureau of the Census, U.S. Department of Commerce.

1993a   Census 2000 Updates, Year 2000 Research and Development Staff (February-May). Bureau of the Census, U.S. Department of Commerce.

1993b   Design Alternative Recommendation #14, Year 2000 Research and Development Staff (May 17, 1993). Bureau of the Census, U.S. Department of Commerce.

1993c   Design Alternative Recommendation #3, Year 2000 Research and Development Staff (May 17, 1993). Bureau of the Census, U.S. Department of Commerce.

1993d   Design Alternative Recommendation #2, Year 2000 Research and Development Staff (May 17, 1993). Bureau of the Census, U.S. Department of Commerce.

1993e   Design Alternative Recommendations, Year 2000 Research and Development Staff (May 17, 1993). Bureau of the Census, U.S. Department of Commerce.

1993f   Summary of Research Projects, prepared by the Special Methods Working Group (April 26, 1993). Bureau of the Census, U.S. Department of Commerce.

1993g   Year 2000 Proposed Special Methods Projects: FY 1993-94, prepared by the Special Methods Working Group (March 18, 1993). Bureau of the Census, U.S. Department of Commerce.

Citro, Constance F., and Michael L. Cohen, eds.

1985   *The Bicentennial Census: New Directions for Census Methodology in 1990.* Panel on Decennial Census Methodology, Committee on

National Statistics, National Research Council. Washington, D.C.: National Academy Press.

Coale, A.J.
1955   The population of the United States in 1950 classified by age, sex, and color--a revision of census figures. *Journal of the American Statistical Association* 50:16-54.

Committee on National Statistics
1978   *Counting the People in 1980: An Appraisal of Census Plans*. Panel on Decennial Census Plans, Committee on National Statistics, National Research Council. Washington, D.C.: National Academy of Sciences.

1992   Letter Report to the Bureau of the Census from the Panel to Evaluate Alternative Census Methods, Committee on National Statistics, Commission on Behavioral and Social Sciences and Education. National Research Council, Washington, D.C.

1993   *Planning The Decennial Census: Interim Report*. Panel on Census Requirements in the Year 2000 and Beyond, Committee on National Statistics, National Research Council. Washington, D.C.: National Academy of Sciences.

de la Puente, Manuel
1993   Why Are People Missed or Erroneously Included by the Census: A Summary of Findings from Ethnographic Coverage Reports. Report prepared for the Advisory Committee for the Design of the Year 2000 Census Meeting, March 5. Bureau of the Census, U.S. Department of Commerce.

Duncan, George T., Thomas B. Jabine, and Virginia de Wolf, editors
1993   *Private Lives and Public Policies: Confidentiality and Accessibility of Government Statistics*. Panel on Confidentiality and Data Access, Committee on National Statistics, National Research Council. Washington, D.C.: National Academy Press.

Ericksen, E. P., L.F. Estrada, J.W. Tukey, and K.M. Wolter
1991   Report on the 1990 Decennial Census and the Post-Enumeration Survey. Report of the Special Advisory Panel to the Secretary of the U. S. Department of Commerce (June 21, 1991).

Ferrari, Pamela W., and L. Bailey
1983   The 1980 Census Telephone Follow-up Experiment--Preliminary Assessments and Implications. Unpublished paper. Bureau of the Census, U.S. Department of Commerce.

Goldfield, Edwin D.
1992   Innovations in the Decennial Census of Population and Housing: 1940-1990. Paper prepared for the Committee on National Statistics, Commission on Behavioral and Social Sciences and Education, National Research Council.

Griffin, Richard, and A. Cresce

1993   Results from Scoping Meeting for the Matrix Sampling Joint
        Application Development (JAD) Workshop. Bureau of the Census,
        U.S. Department of Commerce.

Hansen, M.H., W.N. Hurwitz, and M.A. Bershad
1961   Measurement errors in censuses and surveys. *Bulletin of the
        International Statistical Institute* 38, II.

Herriot, R.A., D.V. Bateman, and W.F. McCarthy
1989   The decade census program--a new approach for meeting the nation's
        needs for sub-national data. *American Statistical Association
        Proceedings, Section on Social Statistics*. Alexandria, Va.: American
        Statistical Association.

Himes, C.L., and Clogg, C.C.
1992   An overview of demographic analysis as a method for evaluating census
        coverage in the United States. *Population Index* 58:587-607.

Hogan, Howard
1992   The 1990 Post-Enumeration Survey: An overview. *The American
        Statistician* 46(4):261-269.

1993   The 1990 Post-Enumeration Survey: Operations and results. *Journal
        of the American Statistical Association* 88(423):1047-1060.

Horvitz, Daniel G.
1986   Statement to the Subcommittee on Census and Population, U.S. House
        of Representatives (May 1). Research Triangle Institute, Research
        Triangle Park, N.C.

Isaki, C.T., J.H. Tsay, and Y. Thibaudeau
1993   Evaluation of Two Sample Design Options for Sampling for the Count.
        2KS Memorandum Series Design 2000, Book 1, Chapter 12, #1 (May
        12, 1993). Bureau of the Census, U.S. Department of Commerce.

Kish, L.
1981   *Using Cumulated Rolling Samples*. No. 80-52810. Washington, D.C.:
        U.S. Government Printing Office.

1990   Rolling samples and censuses. *Survey Methodology* 16:63-71.

Lee, Margaret M.
1993   *Legal Issues for Census 2000*. Congressional Research Service Report
        93-177-A. Washington, D.C.: U.S. Government Printing Office.

McKenney, N.R., and A.R. Cresce
1992   Measurement of Ethnicity in the United States: Experiences of the
        U.S. Census Bureau. Paper presented at the Joint Canada-United
        States Conference on the Measurement of Ethnicity, Ottawa, April 1-3.

McLaughlin, Joseph M.
1993   Transcript of the New York City judge's decision in favor of Secretary
        of Commerce Mosbacher's decision not to adjust the 1990 census
        population counts (April). Memorandum and order 88CV3474,
        92CV1566.92CV2037.

Miskura, Susan

1993a   Alternative Matrix Sampling Plans. Bureau of the Census, U.S. Department of Commerce (March 12).

1993b   Definition, Clarification and Issues: One Number Census. Bureau of the Census, U.S. Department of Commerce (April 14).

Mulry, Mary H.
1992   Overview of Coverage Measurement Methodologies. Bureau of the Census, U.S. Department of Commerce (December 14).

Mulry, Mary H., and B.D. Spencer
1991   Total error in PES estimates of population (with discussion). *Journal of the American Statistical Association* 86:839-844.

1993   Accuracy of the 1990 census and undercount adjustments. *The Journal of the American Statistical Association* 88(423):1080-1091.

Newhouse, Jr., Q.
1992   *Small Area Studies of 1990 Census Outreach Efforts Among Asian and Pacific Islander Americans, American Indians and Alaska Natives: Summary of Results.* 1990 Decennial Census Preliminary Research and Evaluation Memorandum No. 194. Bureau of the Census. Washington, D.C.: U.S. Department of Commerce.

Ogden Government Services and IDC Government
1993   U.S. Bureau of the Census Technology Assessment of Data Collection Technologies for the Year 2000. First Technology Assessment Report prepared for the Year 2000 Staff. (Contract GSOOK90AJD0621) Bureau of the Census, U.S. Department of Commerce.

Romero, Mary
1992   Ethnographic Evaluation of Behavioral Causes of Census Undercount of Undocumented Immigrants and Salvadorans in the Mission District of San Francisco, California. Ethnographic Evaluation of the 1990 Decennial Census Report #18. Paper prepared under Joint Statistical Agreement 89-41 with the San Francisco State University Foundation. Bureau of the Census, U.S. Department of Commerce.

Sailer, Peter., B. Windheim, and E. Yau
1993   How Well Can IRS Count the Population? Handout prepared for a meeting of the Washington Statistical Society in Washington, D.C., June 8. Statistics of Income Division, Internal Revenue Service, U.S. Department of Treasury.

Scarr, Harry A.
1993   Planning for the 2000 Census. Written testimony of Harry Scarr, acting director, Bureau of the Census, U.S. Department of Commerce. Presented before the Subcommittee on Census, Statistics, and Postal Personnel, Committee on Post Office and Civil Service, May 27.

Standish, Linda, R. Bender, M. Michalowski, and A. Peters
1993   Administrative Record Comparison (ARC): Report on Demographic Comparisons with the 1991 Canadian Census. Paper prepared for 1993 Annual Research Conference, Bureau of the Census, March 21-24.

Statistics Canada.

Starr, W.A.
    1992   *Information from 1990 Census Telephone Questionnaire Assistance Records (D-399s).* 1990 Decennial Census Preliminary Research and Evaluation Memorandum No. 194. Washington, D.C.: Bureau of the Census.

U.S. Department Health and Human Services
    1976   *The Objectives of the SSA.* OHR/EC Publication No. 029 (7-76). Washington, D.C.: U.S. Department of the Treasury.

U.S. General Accounting Office
    1992   *Decennial Census: 1990 Results Show Need for Fundamental Reform.* Washington, D.C.: U.S. Government Printing Office.

APPENDIX

BIOGRAPHICAL SKETCHES OF PANEL MEMBERS AND STAFF

NORMAN M. BRADBURN is the Tiffany and Margaret Blake Distinguished Service Professor in the Department of Psychology and the Harris Graduate School of Public Policy Studies at the University of Chicago and senior vice-president for Research at the National Opinion Research Center. He is an authority on nonsampling errors in surveys and has written extensively on questionnaire design. He has been active in the developing field of research applying cognitive psychological principles to the study of response errors in surveys.

ROBERT M. BELL is a statistician with the RAND Corporation. He has worked on a number of different projects mainly in health and education. His areas of expertise include survey design, survey analysis, and general experimental design issues.

GORDON J. BRACKSTONE is assistant chief statistician responsible for statistical methodology, computing, and geography at Statistics Canada. His professional work has been in survey methodology, particularly the assessment of the quality of census and survey data. He is a fellow of the American Statistical Association and an elected member of the Inernational Statistical Institute.

CLIFFORD C. CLOGG is a demographer and statistician at Pennsylvania State University. He is chair of the Committee on Population Statistics of the Population Association of America, a member of the Census Advisory Committee, and was the coordinating and applications editor of the *Journal of the American Statistical Association*. His areas of specialization are categorical data analysis and social statistics.

THOMAS B. JABINE is a statistical consultant who specializes in the areas of sampling, survey research methods, and statistical policy. He was formerly statistical policy expert for the Energy Information Administration, chief mathematical statistician for the Social Security Administration, and chief of the Statistical Research Division of the Bureau of the Census. He is a fellow of the American Statistical Association and a member of the International Statistical Institute.

KATHERINE S. NEWMAN is a professor of anthropology at Columbia University. Her areas of specialization include social anthropology and American society, anthropology and public policy, and legal and political anthropology. She has been studying downward mobility in terms of political, economic, and family aspects.

D. BRUCE PETRIE is assistant chief statistician of the Social, Institutions, and Labor Statistics Field at Statistics Canada. He is responsible for social statistics, which includes the census of population, household surveys, and Canada's equivalent of the Current Population Survey.

PETER A. ROGERSON is professor and chair of geography at the State University of New York, Buffalo. His areas of specialization include internal migration, mathematical demography, and estimates and projections. He was formerly a research trainee at the Census Bureau in the Census Bureau/American Statistical Association program on economic-demographic modeling

KEITH F. RUST is an associate director at Westat, Inc., and formerly was with the Australian Bureau of Statistics. His work deals mainly with educational surveys, particularly the National Assessment of Educational Progress. His areas of specialization include survey research and data analysis.

NORA CATE SCHAEFFER is an associate professor of sociology at the University of Wisconsin, Madison. Her areas of expertise include respondent behavior and interviewer-respondent interaction. Her past research has concentrated on a number of different areas in survey methodology dealing with nonsamping error, both nonresponse and response errors of various kinds. She is on the editorial board of *Public Opinion Quarterly*, *Sociological Methodology*, and *Sociological Methods Research*.

EDWARD A. SCHILLMOELLER is senior vice president of the A.C. Nielsen Company, where he directs all statistical operations and activities of the media research division. His work includes both continuous and ad hoc household surveys of television audiences. His interests are sample design and survey methods.

DUANE L. STEFFEY is a study director with the Committee on National Statistics, National Research Council. He is on leave from San Diego State University, where he is an associate professor of mathematical sciences. He has published research on statistical methods, particularly on hierarchical Bayesian modeling, and has engaged broadly in interdisciplinary research and consulting.

MICHAEL F. WEEKS is senior study director at the Center for Survey Research of the Research Triangle Institute. His areas of expertise include survey methods and operations. In particular, he is interested in survey methods aimed at reducing nonsampling error and making survey operations more efficient and more cost-effective.

ALAN M. ZASLAVSKY is an assistant professor of statistics at Harvard University.

He has studied methods for estimating and correcting census undercount, and his research interests include the application of hierarchical Bayes methods for combining different sources of data.

DATE DUE

NATIONAL ACADEMY PRESS

The National Academy Press was created by the
National Academy of Sciences to publish the reports
issued by the Academy and by the National Academy
of Engineering, the Institute of Medicine, and the
National Research Council, all operating under the
charter granted to the National Academy of Sciences
by the Congress of the United States.

ISBN 0-309-04979-2